Road Transport Operation

Case Law Review

Michael Jewell

Croner Publications Ltd
Croner House
London Road
Kingston upon Thames
Surrey KT2 6SR
Telephone: 0181-547 3333

Copyright © 1997 Croner Publications Ltd

Published by
Croner Publications Ltd
Croner House
London Road
Kingston upon Thames
Surrey KT2 6SR
Tel: 0181-547 3333

All rights reserved.
No part of this publication may be reproduced,
stored in a retrieval system, or transmitted in any form or by
any means, electronic, mechanical, photocopying, recording
or otherwise, without the prior permission of
Croner Publications Ltd.

While every care has been taken
in the writing and editing of this book,
readers should be aware that only Acts of Parliament
and Statutory Instruments have the force of law,
and that only the courts can authoritatively
interpret the law.

British Library Cataloguing-in-Publication Data.
A catalogue record for this book
is available from the British Library.

ISBN 1 85524 400 4

Printed by Creative Print and Design Group, Wales.

INTRODUCTION

The aim of this publication is to bring together into a handy pocketbook some of the main case law reports relevant to the road haulage industry.

Three main topics are covered: drivers' hours and tachographs (12 cases), operator's licensing (1 case) and overloading (6 cases).

The cases are from the European Court, the High Court of Justice (Queen's Bench Division) and the Court of Appeal (Criminal Division).

The drivers' hours and tachograph cases include:
- the meaning of the "last day of the previous week" (case 1)
- driving periods and breaks (case 2)
- the period of 24 hours with reference to drivers' daily rest (case 3)
- the daily working period (case 4)
- emergency departures from the drivers' hours rules (case 5)
- knowledge is necessary to prove the offences of causing and permitting breaches of the drivers' hours rules (case 6)
- defining "roads open to the public" for the purpose of the drivers' hours regulations (case 7)
- timing drivers' work and rest periods (case 8)
- wilful ignorance is not "causing an offence" (case 9)
- permitting drivers' hours offences (case 10)
- defining "permissible maximum weight" for installation of the tachograph (case 11)

- falsification of tachograph charts abroad — an offence under the Forgery and Counterfeiting Act 1981 (case 12).

The operator's licensing case covers the question of exemption for emergency vehicles (case 13).

The overloading of vehicles cases cover:
- separate offences created for each permitted weight exceeded (case 14)
- regulation 80(1) and (2) do not create separate offences (case 15)
- evidence that computerised weighbridges are working properly (case 16)
- entitlement to rely on the Certificate of Weight (case 17)
- the owner of a vehicle is not the "user" of the vehicle when it is driven by a self-employed driver (case 18)
- it is not necessary to prove that the *Code of Practice for Dynamic Axle Weighers* has been complied with (case 19).

Legal terms have been explained wherever they occur in the text.

CONTENTS

DRIVERS' HOURS AND TACHOGRAPHS

EUROPEAN COURT

Case 1: Meaning of "Last Day of Previous Week"   1
Case 2: Driving Periods and Breaks   5
Case 3: Period of 24 Hours and Journeys to Countries Not Party to AETR   9
Case 4: Daily Working Period   15
Case 5: Emergency Departures from Drivers' Hours Rules   21

HIGH COURT OF JUSTICE (QUEEN'S BENCH DIVISION)

Case 6: Knowledge is Necessary for the Offences of Causing and Permitting Breaches of the Drivers' Hours Rules   23
Case 7: "Roads Open to the Public" for the Purposes of the Drivers' Hours and Tachograph Regulations are Roads to Which the Public Have Access   31
Case 8: Timing Drivers' Work and Rest Periods   37
Case 9: Wilful Ignorance is Not "Causing an Offence"   41
Case 10: Permitting Drivers' Hours Offences   43
Case 11: "Permissible Maximum Weight" Means "Gross Weight of Vehicle and Trailer"   49

COURT OF APPEAL (CRIMINAL DIVISION)

Case 12: Drivers Who Falsify Tachograph Records Abroad and Then Produce Them are Guilty of an Offence Under the Forgery and Counterfeiting Act 1981   51

OPERATORS' LICENSING

HIGH COURT OF JUSTICE (QUEEN'S BENCH DIVISION)

Case 13: Operator's Licensing Exemption for Emergency Vehicles   55

OVERLOADING

HIGH COURT OF JUSTICE (QUEEN'S BENCH DIVISION)

Case 14: Separate Offences Created for Each Permitted Weight Exceeded   57

Case 15: Regulation 80(1) and (2) Do Not Create Separate Offences   63
Case 16: Evidence That Computerised Weighbridges are Working Properly 65
Case 17: Entitled to Rely Upon Certificate of Weight   67
Case 18: Owner Does Not "Use" Vehicle When it is Driven by Self-employed Driver 71
Case 19: It is Not Necessary to Prove That the *Code of Practice for Dynamic Axle Weighers* Has Been Complied With to Obtain an Overloading Conviction 83

DRIVERS' HOURS AND TACHOGRAPHS

EUROPEAN COURT

CASE 1: MEANING OF "LAST DAY OF PREVIOUS WEEK"

Mario Nijs and Transport Van Schoonbeek-Matterne NV (13 December 1991)
The European Court ruled that the phrase "the last day of the previous week on which he drove", used in Article 15(7) of Council Regulation (EEC) No.3821/85, of 20 December 1985 on recording equipment in road transport, refers to the last driving day of the last week, prior to the current week, during which the driver concerned drove a vehicle subject to Council Regulation (EEC) No.3820/85, of 20 December 1985 on the harmonisation of certain social legislation relating to road transport.

Politierechtbank te Hasselt (Belgium) had asked the Court for a preliminary ruling on two questions relating to the interpretation of Article 15(7) of Regulation No. 3821/85. Those questions arose in the course of criminal proceedings against Mario Nijs, a driver employed by the firm Transport van Schoonbeek-Matterne NV. As the driver of a vehicle subject to recording equipment regulations, Mr Nijs was charged, among other things, with having been unable to produce, when requested by an authorised inspecting officer, all the record sheets used during the current week and the record sheet for the last day of the previous week on which he drove as required under Article 15(7) of Regulation No. 3821/85 and Article 2 of Belgian Law of 18 February 1969 enacting it.

In its judgment, the European Court said that Article 15(7) of Regulation No. 3821/85 provided:

Whenever requested by an authorised inspecting officer to do so, the driver must be able to produce record sheets for the current week, and in any case for the last day of the previous week in which he drove.

Article 1(4) of Regulation No. 3820/85, to which Article 2 of Regulation No. 3821/85 referred for its definition of terms, defined "week" as being "the period between 00.00 hours on Monday and 24.00 hours on Sunday".

Mr Nijs was on holiday from Thursday 27 July to Sunday 6 August 1989 and returned to work on Monday 7 August. On Thursday 10 August, the day on which he was subjected to a roadside check, Mr Nijs had not entered his name on the current record sheet and did not have any record sheets with him for previous driving periods.

Politierechtbank te Hasselt asked the following questions.
1. What is the meaning of the phrase "the last day of the previous week on which he drove" in Article 15(7) of Regulation No. 3821/85? Is that day the last calendar day, the last working day or the last driving day of that week?
2. Does the "previous week" mean the week directly preceding the inspection or any week preceding the inspection in which the driver drove a vehicle subject to the relevant EEC regulations?

The national court took the view that the French version of Article 15(7) of Regulation No. 3821/85 clearly showed the relevant day to be the last one on which the driver drove, while the Dutch version allowed other interpretations, such as: the last calendar day of the last week in which the driver drove, the last working day of that same week, or the last calendar day or the last working day of the week immediately prior to the inspection. Among the other language versions it should be noted that some, such as the Italian and Spanish, suggested that the relevant day was the last day of the previous week in which the driver drove, whereas the English version referred to the last day of driving and not to the last day of a week in which the driver drove.

The Court had consistently held that in the case of divergence between the different language versions of a Community text, the provision in question must be interpreted by reference to the purpose and general scheme of the rules of which it formed a part.

In order to improve working conditions and safety in road transport, Regulation No. 3820/85 laid down precise rules concerning, in particular, driving and rest periods for drivers. To ensure effective monitoring of those rules, Regulation No. 3821/85 required, with certain exceptions, that approved recording equipment be installed and used in all vehicles subject to Regulation 3820/85. Known as a "tachograph", that device was designed to record on approved record sheets, either automatically or semi-automatically, data relating to driving and other working periods of drivers and their daily and weekly periods of availability and rest.

Under Article 15(2) of Regulation No. 3821/85, drivers must use the record sheets on every day which they drive, starting from the moment they take over the vehicle. The rules in question, therefore, did not require such a sheet to be used on a day without driving.

It followed that effective monitoring required the driver to produce such a sheet for the last driving day of the last week in which he or she drove prior to the inspection, in order to check compliance with the compulsory weekly rest period. If the driver was not driving in the week prior to that in which the inspection took place, or if he or she was not driving on the last calendar day or the last working day of the last week in which he or she was driving, the objectives of the rules in question did not require the driver to produce the record sheet for those respective periods.

It followed that, in answer to the questions referred by the national court, the phrase "the last day of the previous week on which he drove" used in Article 15(7) of Regulation No. 3821/85 referred to the last driving day of the last week, prior to the current week, during which the driver concerned drove a vehicle subject to Regulation No. 3820/85.

CASE 2: DRIVING PERIODS AND BREAKS

Kevin Albert Charlton, James Huyton and Raymond Edward William Wilson (15 December 1993)

The European Court ruled that Article 7(1) and (2) of Council Regulation (EEC) No. 3820/85, of 20 December 1985 on the harmonisation of certain social legislation relating to road transport, is to be interpreted as prohibiting drivers to which it applies from driving continuously for more than 4½ hours. But where a driver has taken 45 minutes' break either as a single break or as several breaks of at least 15 minutes during or at the end of a 4½ hour period, the calculation provided for by Article 7(1) of Regulation No. 3820/85 should begin afresh, without taking into account the driving time and breaks previously completed by the driver. The calculation provided for by Article 7(1) begins at the moment when the driver sets in motion the recording equipment provided for by Council Regulation (EEC) No. 3821/85, of 20 December 1985 on recording equipment in road transport, and begins driving.

Manchester Crown Court had asked the European Court for a preliminary ruling on the interpretation of Article 7(1) and (2) of Regulation No. 3820/85, after Kevin Charlton, transport manager of Lovers Lane Transport, Lancashire haulier Raymond Wilson and lorry driver James Huyton had appealed against their convictions by Heywood magistrates on offences involving breaches of the 4½ hour driving rule.

Interpreting the Regulation

In its judgment, the European Court said that Article 7 provided the following.
1. After 4½ hours' driving, the driver shall observe a break of at least 45 minutes, unless he or she begins a rest period.
2. This break may be replaced by breaks of at least 15 minutes each distributed over the driving period or immediately after this period in such a way as to comply with the provisions of paragraph 1.

Regulation No. 3820/85 repealed and replaced Council Regulation (EEC) No. 543/69, of 25 March 1969 on the harmonisation of certain social legislation concerning road transport. It was intended to make the relevant provisions more flexible without undermining their objectives. Its aim was to:
- eliminate disparities which distorted competition
- preserve road safety

- improve the living and working conditions of drivers.

It replaced the flexible week by a fixed week (Article 1(4)).

As regards driving periods, Regulation No. 3820/85 continued to limit the period of continuous driving (Article 7(1)) and the daily driving period (Article 6(1)), but lengthened those periods by comparison with Regulation No. 643/69. At the same time the breaks from driving were adjusted to take account of the longer daily driving period. Article 11 of Regulation No. 3820/85 authorised Member States to apply stricter rules with respect to driving periods. To enable drivers to reach a suitable stopping place, Article 12 allowed them to depart from the provisions of the Regulation to the extent necessary to ensure the safety of persons and the vehicle or its load, provided that road safety was not thereby jeopardised.

The accused in the main proceedings pointed to the ambiguous nature of those provisions, suggesting that the Court should adopt the least restrictive interpretation in accordance with the general principles of law, in particular the principles requiring the interpretation that was most favourable to the accused in criminal proceedings and the interpretation which gave the greatest freedom to individuals to conduct their affairs as they saw fit. The Court concluded that the daily driving period comprised two 4½ hour periods, within or at the end of which the driver took a break of 45 minutes or several breaks of at least 15 minutes totalling 45 minutes. Since the break relating to the second 4½ hour period might be taken at the end of that period, the Regulation permitted the driver to drive for 9 hours each day, stopping for only 45 minutes at any moment within or at the end of the first 4½ hour period (the "wipe the slate clean" interpretation).

The UK took the opposite view. In its opinion, the interpretation proposed by the accused would allow a driver who concentrated his or her breaks relating to the first 4½ hour period at the beginning of the day to drive continuously almost all day. Such a solution would run counter to the Regulation, which in no circumstances permitted driving for more than 4½ hours without taking one or more breaks totalling 45 minutes. Consequently, in the UK's view, within the maximum daily driving period of 9 hours, the driver must, in order to comply with Article 7 of the Regulation, take account at all times not only of the period during which he or she intended to drive but also of the period which he or she had already spent at the wheel without taking one or more breaks totalling 45 minutes, so that at the end of the daily driving period of 9 hours there was no period within which the period of driving exceeded 4½ hours (the "rolling period" interpretation).

Finally, France proposed an intermediate solution. According to its interpretation of Article 7 of Regulation No. 3820/85, after 45 minutes' break comprising all the breaks of at least 15 minutes within a 4½ hour driving period, the calculation provided for by Article 7(1) began afresh without taking into account all the previous period.

According to the views put forward by the UK and France, the daily driving period provided for by Article 6(1) of the Regulation did not, as the accused claimed, consist of two 4½ hour periods. According to UK's interpretation, Article 7(1) of the Regulation solely laid down an obligation to take breaks at any time within the daily driving period. France's view did not preclude the possibility that the calculation of the 4½ hours provided for by Article 7(1) of the Regulation might recommence several times within a daily driving period.

The Court held that where a provision was insufficiently clear and explicit, its scope should be determined by examining its objectives and the legal context in which it was situated.

The preamble to Regulation No. 3820/85 showed that the limits set on driving times were intended to serve the interests of road safety. That was confirmed by Article 12 of the Regulation, which allowed a driver to depart from the provisions of the Regulation, including Article 7, in order to enable him or her to reach a suitable stopping place, provided that road safety was not thereby jeopardised.

It followed that Article 7(1) and (2) of Regulation No. 3820/85 could not be interpreted as authorising drivers to drive continuously for a period of more than 4½ hours.

The interpretation advocated by the accused must therefore be rejected, since it did not conform to the objectives of road safety pursued by Regulation No. 3820/85.

The Court also noted that Regulation No. 3820/85 made more flexible the provisions of Regulation No. 543/69, including the weekly and daily limits on driving periods and the rest periods. Regulation No. 3820/85 lengthened the driving periods provided for by Articles 6(1) and 7(1) but at the same time lengthened the break provided for by Article 7(1) and (2).

In that context, any stricter limit on driving time must be seen as an exception to the general objective pursued by Regulation No. 3820/85 of making the provisions more flexible and must therefore be interpreted narrowly.

The interpretation advocated by the UK was contrary to the objective of making the provisions of Regulation No. 543/69 more flexible. The calculation which it proposed to determine the breaks would end only on the expiry of the daily driving period or when the driver had taken a break of at least 45 minutes. That would lead in fact to the same driving period being counted twice where a driver divided the compulsory break. Moreover, it was not consistent with the actual wording of Article 7(2) of Regulation No. 3820/85, which provided expressly that the 45 minute break which must be taken after 4½ hours' driving might be "replaced" by breaks of at least 15 minutes each distributed over the driving period or immediately after that period.

Consequently, it must be concluded that, where a driver had taken 45 minutes' break either as a single break or as several breaks or at least 15 minutes during or at the end of a 4½ hour period, the calculation provided for by Article 7(1) of the Regulation should begin afresh without taking account of the driving time and breaks previously completed by the driver.

When does a driving period begin?

Regarding the question as to the moment when the driving period began, it was noted that one of the objectives pursued by Regulation No. 5820/85 in replacing Regulation No. 543/69 was to improve the control of drivers' work.

The system to guarantee the effectiveness of such control was set up by Regulation No. 3821/85, which stated that the only effective control of driving time and breaks provided for by Article 7(1) and (2) of Regulation No. 3820/85 was that achieved by means of the recording equipment provided for by Regulation No. 3821/85.

Consequently, the calculation provided for by Article 7(1) of Regulation No. 3820/85 must begin at the moment when the driver sets in motion the recording equipment provided for by Regulation No. 3821/85 and begins driving.

CASE 3: PERIOD OF 24 HOURS AND JOURNEYS TO COUNTRIES NOT PARTY TO AETR

Van Swieten BV (2 June 1994)

The European Court ruled that the period of 24 hours within which a driver has to take his or her daily rest period commences at the end of either a weekly or daily rest period when the tachograph is set in motion. If the daily rest period is split, then the 24 hour period commences at the end of the period of rest that lasts a minimum of 8 hours. The Court also ruled that the EC drivers' hours and tachograph regulations apply to vehicles registered in a Member State in the course of journeys to and from third countries which are not parties to the European Agreement Concerning the Work of Crews of Vehicles Engaged in International Road Transport (AETR).

The Arrondissementsrechtbank, Amsterdam, had asked the Court for a preliminary ruling on two questions relating to the interpretation of Articles 2(1) and 8(1) of the Council Regulation (EEC) No. 3820/85, of 20 December 1985 on the harmonisation of certain social legislation in relation to road transport. Those questions arose in the course of criminal proceedings against Van Swieten BV, a Dutch international road transport company, for infringements of the provisions of Community law and Netherlands law relating to rest periods and driving times, after the company had appealed against its conviction by the Kantonrechter (Cantonal Court) Amsterdam.

In the course of an inspection in October 1988, the Dutch authorities discovered that 17 drivers employed by Van Swieten had failed to comply with the rules concerning rest periods and driving times while driving vehicles registered in the Netherlands. The offences concerned compliance with the minimum period of rest to be taken in each period of 24 hours, as laid down by Article 8(1) of Regulation No. 3820/85. They had been committed for the most part in the course of journeys within the Community, but also, in some cases, during journeys to destinations in Switzerland or in transit through that country. Switzerland, a non-member country, was not a party to AETR.

The scope of Regulation No. 3820/85 was defined in Article 2 as follows.
1. This regulation applies to carriage by road within the Community.
2. The European Agreement concerning the Work of Crews of Vehicles Engaged in International Road Transport (AETR) shall apply instead of the present rules to international road transport operations:

- to and/or from third countries which are Contracting Parties to the Agreement, or in transit through such countries, for the whole of the journey where such operations are carried out by vehicles registered in a Member State or in one of the said third countries
- to and/or from a third country which is not a Contracting Party to the Agreement in the case of any journey made within the community where such operations are carried out by vehicles registered in one of those countries.

Since Regulation No. 3820/85 did not expressly apply to journeys made by vehicles registered in a Member State which started or finished in a third country which was not a party to AETR, in such situations the Dutch authorities usually applied the Netherlands rules to the whole of the journey and did not take account of Regulation No. 3820/85.

Article 8(1) of Regulation 3820/85 provided that:

In each period 24 hours, the driver shall have a daily rest period of at least 11 consecutive hours, which may be reduced to a minimum of nine consecutive hours not more than three times in any one week, on condition that the equivalent period of rest be granted as compensation before the end of the following week.

In the Netherlands, the system of monitoring compliance with the daily rest periods laid down by the Regulation was based on the following principles. The point in time which was decisive for establishing the 24 hour period was determined by:

- the time of the road check
- the beginning of the weekly rest period
- the beginning of the (complete) daily rest period.

In addition, for the purpose of determining the 24 hour period in each particular case it was necessary, where the calculation apparently encompassed a rest period within the meaning of Article 8(1) of Regulation No. 3820/85, to carry back the aforementioned point in time until a point was reached when the crew member was not free to dispose of his or her own time.

For Van Swieten it had been argued before the appeal court that Regulation No. 3820/85 was applicable to transport operations to or via Switzerland in respect of that part of the journey which took place within the Community and that the Netherlands' legislation should therefore not have been applied. The company contested the method of control adopted by the Dutch authorities in monitoring compliance with the daily rest periods, maintaining that it was incompatible with Article 8(1) of Regulation No. 3820/85.

It was also maintained that the 24 hour period referred to in Article 8(1) of Regulation No. 3820/85 was a fixed period, and that the first such period in a given week started to run at the end of a weekly rest period. The company relied in support of its arguments on: the English version of the Article; a judgment of the High Court of Justice of 28 April 1988 in the case of *Kelly v Schulman;* and on the first recital in the preamble to the Regulations, which pointed out the need for greater flexibility over the provisions of the previous Regulation, namely Council Regulation (EEC) No. 543/69, of 25 March 1969 on the harmonisation of certain social legislation concerning road transport.

In *Kelly v Schulman*, the Divisional Court ruled that in calculating when the weekly rest period was due, the term "day" in Article 6(1) of Regulation No. 3820/85 meant successive periods of 24 hours beginning with the driver's resumption of driving after his or her weekly rest period. The Court also ruled that every driver had to have a weekly rest period, as defined in Article 8 of the Regulation, once in every week (ie the period between midnight on Sunday and midnight on the following Sunday) and that in certain circumstances the weekly rest period fell to be taken earlier.

Thus:

(a) any driver who, in the course of six consecutive driving periods since his or her last weekly rest, had driven in the aggregate not less than the maximum number of hours permitted by the Regulations in six such periods had to begin a weekly rest immediately on the conclusion of the sixth period, but

(b) any such driver who in those six driving periods had driven for an aggregate of less than the maximum number of hours permitted by the Regulations could postpone the commencement of his or her weekly rest period until the end of the sixth day and drive during the period of postponement provided that he or she did not by so doing increase the aggregate of the hours driven since his or her last weekly rest to a figure exceeding the maximum number of hours permitted by the Regulations in six consecutive daily driving periods.

The European Court were asked the following questions.

1. In regard to Article 2(1) — Must it be interpreted as meaning that the Regulation is (also) applicable to carriage by road within the Community, to or from non-member countries not parties to AETR, or in transit through such countries, using vehicles registered in a Member State?

2. In regard to Article 8(1) — Must the words "each period of 24 hours" be interpreted as meaning that such a period may begin at any time whatsoever depending on the beginning of the weekly and (complete) daily rest period and the time of the on-the-road check, or does the first of one or more successive periods begin at the time when the first weekly rest period ends?

Is Regulation No. 3820/85 applicable in countries not party to AETR?

In its judgment, the European Court said that, in relation to the first question, Article 2(1) of Regulation No. 3820/85 provided that:

> This regulation applies to carriage by road, as defined in Article 1(1), within the Community.

The Regulation, which replaced Regulation No 543/69, provided for the harmonisation of certain social legislation relating to road transport, in particular by laying down rules relating to driving times and rest periods for drivers. The Regulation aimed to safeguard and extend the progress made by its precursor, by making its provisions more flexible but without undermining their objectives.

One of the main objectives of Regulation No. 3820/85, as in the case of Regulation No. 543/69, was the improvement of road safety and working conditions for drivers.

The effectiveness of those rules would be compromised if the application of the European Community system were dependent on the journeys made by vehicles registered in different Member States and if national laws continued to apply where the journeys were made only partly within the Community.

It followed that Regulation No. 3820/85 covered all road transport services operated within the Community by vehicles registered in a Member State, even where the carriage took place partly in non-Member States.

That interpretation was confirmed by the wording of Article 2 of Regulation No. 543/69, according to which that regulation applied "to carriage by road in respect of any journey or part of a journey made within the Community". It was clear from the wording that the Regulation, which preceded Regulation No. 3820/85 and had the same objectives as it, related to all carriage by road within the territory of the Community regardless of the route taken by the vehicle.

This interpretation was also borne out by Article 2(2) of Regulation No. 3820/85. That provision, which set out the cases in which AETR was to apply in place of Regulation No. 3820/85, contained no reference to any case analogous to that raised by the first question submitted for a preliminary ruling. It followed that the present case was governed neither by the AETR nor by national law, but fell within the scope of Regulation No. 3820/85.

The reply to the first question should therefore be that Article 2(1) of Regulation No. 3820/85 must be interpreted as meaning that the Regulation was also applicable to carriage by road within the Community by vehicles registered in a Member State in the course of journeys to or from third countries which were not parties to AETR, or in transit through such countries.

When does a "period of 24 hours" begin?

In regard to the question of the commencement of the "period of 24 hours" referred to in Article 8(1) of Regulation No. 3820/85, it should be noted that the Regulation was intended to ensure road safety and to improve working conditions for drivers.

With that in mind, Article 8(1) of Regulation No. 3820/85 sought, by providing that each period of 24 hours must include a minimum number of hours of rest, to ensure that driving times and rest periods alternated, so that drivers did not remain at the wheel of their vehicles for periods of such length as to cause tiredness and jeopardise road safety.

It followed from that objective that the wording "period of 24 hours" could not be taken to mean an isolated period of time beginning at the same time each day, regardless of the previous daily or weekly rest period. That interpretation, known as the "fixed start" approach, would in some cases allow drivers to remain at the wheel for an excessive period before taking their daily rest, thereby jeopardising road safety.

Thus, the term "period of 24 hours" referred to in Article 8(1) of Regulation No. 3820/85 meant a period whose commencement was variable, in that it began to run at the same time as the actual commencement of driving after the end of the previous daily or weekly rest period. Only by adopting that interpretation was it possible to devise a system of alternating periods of driving and rest which preserved road safety and eased drivers' working conditions.

Given that the second paragraph of Article 8(1) of Regulation No. 3820/85 enabled drivers to divide the daily rest period into two or more separate periods, it was pointed out that the calculation of the period of 24 hours must, in such circumstances, begin at the end of the longest rest period, namely that lasting for a minimum of 8 hours.

The reply to the second question should therefore be that the expression "each period of 24 hours" in Article 8(1) of Regulation No. 3820/85 must be interpreted as meaning any period of 24 hours commencing at the time when the driver activated

DRIVERS' HOURS AND TACHOGRAPHS

the tachograph following a weekly or daily rest period. Where the daily rest was taken in two or three separate periods, the calculation must commence at the end of the period of not less than eight hours.

CASE 4: DAILY WORKING PERIOD

Marc Michielsen and Geybels Transport Services NV (GTS) (9 June 1994)

The European Court ruled that the "daily working period" within the meaning of Article 15(2) of Council Regulation (EEC) No. 3821/85, of 20 December 1985 on recording equipment in road transport, comprises: the driving time; all other periods of work; the period of availability; breaks in work; and, where the driver divides his or her daily rest into two or three separate periods, such a period provided that it does not exceed one hour. The daily working period commences at the time when the driver activates the tachograph following a weekly or daily rest period or, if the daily rest is divided into separate periods, following the rest period of at least eight hours' duration. It ends at the beginning of a daily rest period or, if the daily rest is divided into separate periods, at the beginning of a rest period extending over a minimum of eight consecutive hours. The term "day" within the meaning of Council Regulation (EEC) No. 3820/85, of 20 December 1985 on the harmonisation of certain social legislation in relation to road transport, and of Regulation No. 3821/85, must be understood as equivalent to the term "period of 24 hours", which refers to any period of that duration which commences at the time when the driver activates the tachograph following a weekly or daily rest period.

The Politierechtbank te Hasselt (Belgium) had asked the Court for a preliminary ruling on the interpretation of Articles 6 and 8(1) of Regulation No. 3820/85 and Article 15(2)–(4) inclusive of Regulation No. 3821/85, following questions raised in criminal proceedings against Marc Michielsen and Geybels Transport Service as the party liable at civil law.

In its judgment the European Court said that on 12 August 1991 Michielsen, who was driving a truck and trailer for Geybels Transport, was the subject of an inspection carried out in Antwerp in accordance with both Regulation No. 3820/85 and Regulation No. 3821/85. The inspection disclosed that he had committed several breaches of those Regulations. The documents before the Court showed that he failed on two different days to observe the rest and driving periods and, moreover, on the day of the inspection he had used two record sheets in the tachograph on his vehicle. The point of difficulty still to be resolved by the national court, and for which an interpretation of the relevant Community provisions has been shown to be necessary, concerned the question of Michielsen's fraudulent use of the record sheets.

Michielsen claimed before the Politierechtbank te Hasselt that the use of the record sheet was quite in order since, having completed his daily working period and left the company's premises, he was undertaking a new assignment.

The questions the Court were asked to decide were as follows.
1. *Period of Work* — Is the period of work each period during which the driver of a vehicle subject to both Regulation No. 3820/85 and Regulation No. 3821/85 cannot freely dispose of his or her time? Does the period of work comprise driving periods, breaks in driving and time devoted to other activities? Is that definition sufficiently correct or must it be qualified or replaced by another definition?
2. *Day* — Is a day a period of 24 hours and when does a day commence for the purposes of interpreting Regulation No. 3820/85 and Regulation No. 3821/85: at 00.00 hours of the calendar day or at the moment when the driver first takes over a vehicle subject to those Regulations? Can the day commence at a different time?
3. *End of the working period* — Is the end of the working period the moment at which the driver is no longer accountable for the use of his or her time to the management of the transport company and regains the right to freely dispose of his or her time? Is another definition possible?

What is a "period of work" and when does it end?

The expression "period of work" is to be found in various provisions of Regulation No. 3821/85, and specifically in Article 15(3) and ss.I(a), II(4) and IV(b)(1) of Annex I. However, no definition of that term is provided, in either Regulation No. 3821/85 or Regulation No. 3820/85.

According to the Belgian Government and the European Commission, no definition should be adopted which was derived from Regulation No. 3820/85 and Regulation No. 3821/85, since both measures only partially harmonised social legislation in the road transport sector.

The UK considered that the two Regulations formed a complete system. Consequently, the definitions requested might be deduced from the provisions of those Regulations, and in particular from the term "rest", as defined in Article 1(5) of Regulation No. 3820/85. It therefore considered that "period of work", for the purposes of Article 15(2) of Regulation No. 3821/85, should be taken to mean "the daily working period" since that concept covered the periods during which the driver could not freely dispose of his or her time. The "end of the working period" was thus determined by the start of a sufficient daily or weekly rest period.

For the purpose of giving a helpful reply to the first question put by the national court, it was noted at the outset that the terms "period of work" and "daily working period" might not be regarded as synonymous in the context of Regulation No. 3820/85 and Regulation No. 3821/85. The differences between the two terms emerged from Article 15(2) (3) of Regulation No. 3921/85.

The first paragraph of Article 15(2) of that Regulation provided that "the record sheet should not be withdrawn before the end of the daily working period unless its withdrawal was otherwise authorised".

However, according to the second indent of Article 15(3), the tachograph must enable the following periods of time to be recorded separately and distinctly:

(a) driving time

(b) all other periods of work

(c) other periods of availability

(d) breaks in work and daily rest periods.

It followed from those provisions that the concept of daily working period in Article 15(2) was wider than that of period of work in Article 15(3). The former referred to the entire working day in the sense of an uninterrupted span of time, whereas the latter only covered the times at which the driver was actually engaged in activities having a bearing on driving, including driving time. Consequently, periods of availability and breaks in work and daily rest periods, as mentioned in Article 15(3) of Regulation No. 3821/85, did not fall within the concept of period of work since the fact that those terms were preceded by the term all other periods of work precluded their being regarded as forming part of the period of work.

However, it was not possible to preclude the possibility that the periods of availability and breaks in work and daily rest periods fell within the daily working period since, according to Article 15(2) of Regulation No. 3821/85, they must appear on the record sheet, which might not be withdrawn during the daily working period.

Since the concepts "period of work" and "daily working period" were not synonymous in the context of Regulation No. 3820/85 and Regulation No. 3821/85, it must be determined which of those concepts was referred to by the national court. The only point of difficulty still to be resolved concerned the lawfulness of Michielsen's use of two record sheets in the course of a single day. Given that, according to Article

15(2) of Regulation No. 3821/85, the record sheet might be withdrawn before the end of the daily working period, it was the latter concept, as used in that provision, which must be interpreted in order to enable the national court to determine whether Michielsen's conduct was lawful.

The first question must therefore be understood as referring to the term daily working period, and to its meaning and scope, and must consequently be considered together with the third question, which related to the same problem.

It was necessary, however, to establish which, specifically, of the periods mentioned in Article 15(3) of Regulation No. 3821/85 were covered by the daily working period.

The first two temporal categories (driving time and all other periods of work) were by definition working periods.

In the case of the third category (the period of availability), in view of the fact that pursuant to Article 15(4) of Regulation No. 3821/85 this category may, at the discretion of the Member States, be recorded together with the second category (all other periods of work), it might become impossible at the time of inspection to calculate it independently of the periods of actual work.

With regard to rest periods, it was noted that Article 6(1) of Regulation No 3820/85 fixed the maximum length of the daily driving period. Similarly, the minimum length of the daily rest period was prescribed in Article 8(1) of that Regulation which provided that when the rest was taken in 2 or 3 separate periods during the same 24 hour period, 1 of those periods must be of at least 8 consecutive hours, in which case the minimum length of the rest was to be increased to 12 hours.

Article 1(5) of Regulation No. 3820/85 defined rest as "any uninterrupted period of at least one hour during which the driver might freely dispose of his time". Pursuant to Article 2 of Regulation No. 3821/85, that definition also applied for the purposes of that Regulation.

It followed from the definition of rest laid down in Article 1(5) of Regulation No. 3820/85 that if a driver divided his or her rest into two or three separate periods, any of those periods which was less than one hour in length fell within the daily working period.

With regard to breaks in driving, Article 7(5) of Regulation No. 3820/85 provided that they might not be regarded as daily rest periods. Since, by definition, they must occur between driving periods, they were not capable of being identified individually within the daily working period.

The starting point, for the purpose of determining when the daily working period began and ended, was to be found in the judgment of the European Court of 2 June 1994 in *Van Swieten* (Case C313/92) (see *Case 3: Period of 24 Hours and Journeys to Countries not party to AETR*) in which the court held that the driver's daily period of activity commenced at the time when he or she activated the tachograph following a weekly or daily rest period. If the daily rest was taken in two or three separate periods, the period of activity began at the end of the rest period of at least eight hours' duration. Consequently, the end of the daily working period coincided with the beginning of a daily rest period or, if the daily rest was taken in two or three separate periods, at the beginning of the rest period extending over a minimum of eight consecutive hours.

Thus, the daily working period within the meaning of Article 15(2) of Regulation No. 3821/85, comprised: the driving time; all other periods of work; the period of availability; breaks in work; and, where the driver divided his or her daily rest into two or three separate periods, such a period of rest, provided that it did not exceed one hour. The daily working period commenced at the time when the driver activated the tachograph following a weekly or daily rest period or, where the daily rest was divided into separate periods, following the rest period of at least eight hours' duration. It ended at the beginning of a daily rest period or, in cases where the daily rest was divided into separate periods, at the beginning of a rest period extending over a minimum of eight consecutive hours.

What is a "day"?

By its second question the national court asked whether the concept of "day" within the meaning of Regulation No. 3820/85 and Regulation No. 3821/85 coincided with that of the "period of 24 hours" referred to in Article 8(1) of Regulation No. 3820/85, and when it commenced.

A reading of Article 8(1) of Regulation No. 3820/85 showed that the expressions day and period of 24 hours were synonymous. In the first subparagraph of Article 8(1) reference was made to the period of 24 hours, while in the second the word day was used, the subject of both subparagraphs being the same, namely rest periods.

In its judgment in *Van Swieten*, the Court defined the expression period of 24 hours as meaning the period commencing at the time when the driver activated the tachograph following a weekly or daily rest period.

DRIVERS' HOURS AND TACHOGRAPHS

The reply to the second question should therefore be that the term day within the meaning of Regulation No. 3820/85 and Regulation No. 3821/85 must be understood as equivalent to the term period of 24 hours which referred to any period of that duration which commenced at the time when the driver activated the tachograph following a weekly or daily rest period.

CASE 5: EMERGENCY DEPARTURES FROM DRIVERS' HOURS RULES

Alan Geoffrey Bird (9 November 1995)

The European Court ruled that drivers of vehicles carrying high security loads cannot depart from the drivers' hours rules to get to a secure stopping place when it is known that the journey could not be undertaken within the hours' limits before the driver sets out.

Bolton Crown Court had asked the European Court for an interpretation of the exemption to the drivers' hours rules contained in Article 12 of Council Regulation (EEC) No. 3820/85, of 20 December 1985 on the harmonisation of certain social legislation in relation to road transport, after lorry driver Alan Bird had appealed against his conviction by Rochdale magistrates on sample offences of exceeding the daily driving limit and driving for 4½ hours without the required break. Bird had driven for 5 hours 15 minutes without 45 minutes break when carrying bonded goods on a journey between Dunfermline and Rochdale, and for a total of 10 hours 40 minutes when carrying similar goods between Essex and Immingham. In both cases Bird and his employer had known that it was not possible to comply with the hours provisions before the journeys commenced.

Judge David Hodson had concluded that the derogation in Article 12 was unclear. It read as follows:

> *Provided that road safety is not thereby jeopardised and to enable him to reach a suitable stopping place, the driver may depart from the provisions of this Regulation to the extent necessary to ensure the safety of persons, of the vehicle or of its load. The driver shall indicate the nature of and reason for his departure from those provisions on the record sheet of the recording equipment or in his duty roster.*

In its judgment, the European Court said that it was common ground that the goods were of high value and that road safety was not jeopardised. The essence of the question raised was whether Article 12 authorised a driver to derogate from the provisions of Articles 6, 7 or 8 of the Regulation for reasons known before the journey commenced.

In the present case, the derogation provided for in Article 12 was intended to ensure the safety of persons and of the vehicle and its load. It was clear from the wording that it was only the driver who enjoyed the possibility of derogating from the

Regulation. The provision did not, therefore, extend to the driver's employer, as would be the case if the driver and his or her employer were able to agree before the journey commenced not to comply with the Regulation.

Again, under Article 12, it was for the driver to decide whether it was necessary to derogate from the Regulation, to choose a suitable stopping place and to indicate the nature of and reason for the derogation on either the record sheet of the recording equipment or his or her duty roster. It was clear from such details that only cases where it unexpectedly became impossible to comply with the Regulation during the course of the journey were envisaged.

Furthermore, Article 12 authorised derogations only on condition that road safety was not jeopardised. Before a journey commenced neither drivers nor employers were in a position to say whether that condition would be fulfilled. It was when an unforeseen event occurred, capable of justifying a derogation from the Regulation, that the driver must take into account the requirement of ensuring road safety.

As part of the overall context of Article 12, Article 15(1) of the Regulation required transport undertakings (companies) to organise work in such a way that drivers were able to comply with the Regulation. Such a provision precluded an undertaking from planning a derogation before the driver left.

Finally, the Regulation sought to improve road safety. It was clear that the improvement of road safety was the reason for the strict limitations imposed on driving periods by the Regulation. That aim would not be respected if drivers were allowed to derogate from the Regulation even before the journey commenced.

While it was true that Regulation No. 3820/85 sought to give a degree of flexibility to the provisions of Council Regulation (EEC) No. 543/69, of 25 March 1969 on the Harmonisation of certain social legislation concerning road transport, it was nonetheless clear from the preamble that the legislature did not wish to undermine the objectives of the previous regulation.

HIGH COURT OF JUSTICE (QUEEN'S BENCH DIVISION)

CASE 6: KNOWLEDGE IS NECESSARY FOR THE OFFENCES OF CAUSING AND PERMITTING BREACHES OF THE DRIVERS' HOURS RULES

The Licensing Authority for Goods Vehicles in the Metropolitan Traffic Area v Patrick William Coggins (20 February 1985)

The Queen's Bench Divisional Court ruled that to be guilty of causing or permitting breaches of the drivers' hours regulations the employer has to have guilty knowledge, which is actual or imputed. It also ruled that evidence relating to tachograph records which are not the subject of any summonses is admissible even though it does not fall within the similar fact principle.

The Court dismissed an appeal by the Licensing Authority for the Metropolitan Traffic Area against the decision of the Luton magistrates dismissing charges brought against Patrick William Coggins, trading as P C Transport (Luton), alleging that he had permitted drivers to breach the drivers' hours legislation.

Giving judgment, Mr Justice Taylor said that the defendant had appeared before the Luton magistrates accused of 19 offences of permitting drivers to breach the limits on driving hours and take less than the required amount of rest. Before the prosecuting solicitor opened his case he indicated that he wished to offer no evidence in respect of 7 of the 19 charges, and so those charges were dismissed by the magistrates.

The only witness who gave evidence was then called. That was Mr Kidd, a traffic examiner. He said that in 1983 he had visited the offices of the defendant and had examined a large number of tachograph records covering the defendant's transport operations over a span of several months. In the course of questioning by the prosecution, it was sought to examine him as to individual tachograph records relating to all 19 of the original offences charged and also as to tachograph records in respect of which no summonses had been laid. At that point the defence objected. They contended that evidence concerning the charges which had been dismissed was inadmissable as it was prejudicial to the defendant and it was not within the scope of the similar facts principle. They developed the argument by suggesting that it was inappropriate and contradictory for the prosecution first to offer no evidence on certain charges, inviting the court to dismiss them, and then, by the back door as it were, to bring in evidence in relation to those charges to support the remaining summonses.

On behalf of the prosecution, it was accepted that the evidence was not within the similar facts principle, but it was contended that it was nevertheless admissible and relevant to show that the defendant had prior knowledge of offences being committed. It was therefore necessary to see what the particular charges were against the respondent.

Section 96(11) of the Transport Act 1968 reads as follows.

> If any of the requirements of the domestic drivers' hours code is contravened in the case of any driver (a) that driver; and (b) any other person (being that driver's employer or a person to whose orders that driver was subject) who caused or permitted the contravention, shall be liable on summary conviction to a fine; but a person shall not be liable to be convicted under this subsection if he proves to the court (i) that the contravention was due to unavoidable delay in the completion of a journey arising out of circumstances which he could not reasonably have foreseen; or (ii) in the case of a person charged under paragraph (b) of this subsection, that the contravention was due to the fact that the driver had for any particular period or periods driven or been on duty otherwise than in the employment of that person or, as the case may be, otherwise than in the employment in which he is subject to the orders of that person, and that the person charged was not, and could not reasonably have become, aware of that fact.

The prosecution were saying that the tachograph evidence in relation not only to the charges which stood against the defendant but also to those which had been dismissed was admissible to show that the employer caused or permitted the contravention in each case whereby the driver had exceeded the proper hours and to show that there was prior knowledge of that in the respondent.

The magistrates ruled that the evidence was inadmissible on the grounds that it did not come within the similar facts principle. The prosecution chose initially not to offer the evidence and invited the magistrates to dismiss certain charges. They could not change their decision in order to use the evidence to support the remaining charges. That clearly was a ruling that the evidence was not admissible as a matter of law.

The magistrates went on to say that: "The probative value of the evidence in respect of the dismissed charges was outweighed by its prejudicial value". That was a matter of discretion.

Accordingly, the tachographs were excluded. Mr Kidd, when cross-examined, conceded that he had examined a large number of tachographs (possibly 2,000) and there were only 12 charges remaining against the respondent. That was the end of the evidence. There was then a submission on behalf of the defence that there was no case to answer on the grounds that the prosecution had failed to show any evidence that the defendant had prior knowledge of the offences and that that was an essential element to prove. It was contended that unless there was proof of knowledge then the offences had not been committed.

The defence also pointed out that for an operator which had been operating over several months and had produced as many as 2,000 tachographs, 12 such tachograph records linked to the 12 remaining charges were insufficient from which to infer the necessary guilty knowledge on the part of the respondent.

In reply to that, the prosecution contended that s.96 of the Transport Act 1968 created an offence of absolute liability and therefore knowledge was not required.

The magistrates found the following facts.

> That on the dates and times indicated in each of the twelve informations the relevant tachograph records proved the respective drivers had exceeded the permitted hours, but the prosecution had produced no evidence to show that the defendant or the firm by its responsible officer had any prior knowledge of such breaches.

The magistrates concluded that: first, the offence under s.96(11) or s.96(11)(a) was not an offence of absolute liability; and, second, with no proof of knowledge, the defence submission of no case to answer should be upheld. Accordingly, they dismissed the charges and awarded costs against the prosecution.

The questions which were raised by the case were as follows.
1. Should the magistrates have admitted in evidence driving records completed by employees of the defendant relating to dates earlier than the date of the alleged offence as being evidence from which they might reasonably infer that the defendant permitted the alleged offences?

2. Were the magistrates wrong in law in holding that there was no case to answer upon a submission to that effect, bearing in mind the evidence called by way of the records under s.97(B) of the Transport Act 1968, that was to say the tachograph records showing that the drivers had exceeded the hours alleged?
3. Were the magistrates wrong in law in failing to construe the word "permitted", as used in s.96(11)(a) of the Transport Act 1968, as imposing an absolute liability on the part of the defendant for the relevant offence committed by his employee-driver?

For the appellant it was argued that: first, the offence was one of absolute liability; second, the magistrates were wrong to exclude the other tachograph records; and last, based on the 12 tachograph records before them, the magistrates could not properly come to the conclusion that there was no case to answer, even assuming that knowledge was required in the respondent.

Absolute liability

There was authority contrary to the claim of absolute liability. In subsection (11) of s.96, a defence was provided for the employer under a further subsection (ii) which read as follows.

> *a person shall not be liable to be convicted under this subsection if he proves to the court...in the case of a person charged under paragraph (b) of this subsection, that the contravention was due to the fact that the driver had for any particular period or periods driven or been on duty otherwise than in his employment of that person or, as the case may be, otherwise than in the employment in which he is subject to the orders of that person, and that the person charged was not, and could not reasonably have become, aware of that fact.*

This section was considered in the case of *Knowles Transport Ltd v Russell* (1975). That case was brought under s.96 of the Transport Act 1968 and the question was whether there was evidence from which the magistrates could conclude that the employers knew of the breaches by their drivers. The magistrates had convicted and, on appeal, the contention was that it was not right or logical to find that the company had retrospectively permitted the driver to commit an offence of excessive hours simply because the company could have learnt of the offence after it had been committed, albeit the offence had occurred without the knowledge of some reasonable officer or employee.

It was held that conduct after the occurrence of irregularities was capable of providing a foundation for inferring that a person in effective control of a company in fact had knowledge or means of knowledge when the irregularities occurred. Therefore, in this case there was no foundation for such an inference and as the prosecutor could not establish the element of knowledge required for the offence of permitting, the convictions were quashed.

Mr Justice Melford Stevenson, giving the first judgment in the *Knowles* case, said:

> There is a wealth of authority, and I do not think that I need to refer to it beyond the cases which are named in the case stated, for the proposition that permitting necessitates the proof, and proof by the prosecution in such a case as this, of knowledge on behalf of the individual or company who permits the irregularities to occur. In this case that element is absent and I would therefore allow this appeal.

The appellant referred to the case of *James & Son v Smee* (1955). That was a decision under regulation 101 of the Motor Vehicles (Construction and Use) Regulations 1951. It was a prosecution of an employer for permitting the use of a vehicle in a defective condition. In regulation 101 there was no special defence provided as there is in subsection (11) of s.96 of the Transport Act 1968.

The other authority mentioned in the case of *Knowles* was *Grays Haulage Co. Ltd v Arnold* (1966). That was a prosecution under s.73(1)(c)(ii) of the Road Traffic Act 1960, which was the immediate predecessor to the Transport Act 1968. Section 73(1)(c)(ii) was concerned with the same matter as s.96 of the present Act, but no defence such as that specified in subsection (11)(ii) was to be found.

Mr Justice Taylor had come to the conclusion that the Court ought to follow the decision in *Knowles*. It seemed to him that the mere addition to the 1968 Act of the specific defence in subsection (11)(ii) did not raise any implication that what was previously an offence requiring knowledge of the unlawfulness of an act (*mens rea*) had been converted into an absolute offence.

Had Parliament wished to impose a heavier duty on the employer than had previously existed, then that intention would have been made clear much more directly and a change would have been seen in wording in that part of the section which specifically created the offence rather than having to infer it from the part of the section providing a defence.

If it was said that the provision of the specific defence would be unnecessary unless the intention was to create an otherwise absolute offence, then the answer must be that on occasion Parliament did enact provisions which might seem to be superfluous but which underlined what might not otherwise have been so clearly indicated.

The Court should be extremely wary, in his judgment, of coming to a different conclusion from a previous decision of the Court on a matter which had stood without judicial query for as long as had the decision in *Knowles*.

Recently, in *Regina v Greater Manchester Coroner*, Lord Justice Robert Goff considered this principle in its application to the Divisional Court. He warned against a Divisional Court coming to a different conclusion on a matter of law from a previous Divisional Court except in the most rare cases. The decision in *Knowles* was a decision of a strong three-judge court and he was not prepared to say that the decision was wrong, particularly when the report did not indicate clearly the nature of the arguments addressed by counsel. He had therefore come to the conclusion that the magistrates were right in deciding that this was not an absolute offence and they were not wrong in law in construing the section in the way in which they did.

Were all tachograph records admissible evidence?

The basis of the appeal was that if it was necessary to prove knowledge on the part of the respondent, then the tachograph evidence was admissible on that issue. The difficulty which beset a prosecutor in enforcing the legislation was pointed out. It was easy enough to see whether the driver had committed an offence because the tachograph record revealed that. There was no doubt, in the present case, that each of the surviving charges involved a breach of the law by the driver.

However, if it was necessary, as it was, to prove that an employer had knowledge of the offence in order to permit or cause it, then how could the prosecution prove that other than by looking, over a period, at the way in which an employer conducted its business and establishing whether, after reading what the tachograph records stated over that period, the system was changed, tightened up or anything was done about enforcing the law.

It had been frankly conceded that under the principle of similar facts evidence, the tachograph records, certainly for the period before the offences were charged and for the period during which the offences were charged, would have been admissible. However, the point was that before the magistrates the prosecution had accepted that the evidence they sought to produce was not within the similar facts principle. Once they had accepted that, it was argued that there was no other basis for admitting the evidence. Furthermore, it was argued that they were tied to that concession not only before the magistrates, but also before the Divisional Court.

Mr Justice Taylor could not accept that contention. It seemed to him that the prosecution were merely saying that that evidence was admissible because it showed that the defendant had prior knowledge but that it was not strictly within what was traditionally regarded as the similar fact rule. The traditional context of the similar facts principle had usually involved proof of other criminal acts by the defendant in order to prove some necessary ingredient in the offence charged or in order to rebut some defence. The question, which had always been a vexed one, was usually whether the evidence did truly go to some relevant issue in the case or whether it was simply evidence of an inclination or disposition on the part of the defendant to commit that type of offence.

If the right approach here was to regard the tachograph records as similar fact evidence, then it seemed to Justice Taylor that it would be admissible to prove an important element in the case, namely knowledge on the part of the respondent. Although the tachograph records might prove previous similar offences by the drivers it did not follow that they necessarily showed offences on the part of the respondent. To that extent the disputed evidence was not in the usual "similar facts" mould.

However, Justice Taylor thought that whether that evidence was put in the similar facts category or whether it was simply approached on the basis that it was relevant to an element which required to be proved in the charge, it was either way admissible and the magistrates were wrong to exclude it. He did not think that what was said by the prosecution amounted to a good reason for excluding the evidence before the magistrates and it certainly did not amount to a good reason for resisting the submission before the Court that that evidence should have been admitted. Accordingly, the magistrates should have admitted the evidence of the driving records and they were wrong not to have done so.

Was there a case to answer?

This depended upon the evidence which was actually given. It was submitted that even without the excluded evidence, the tachograph records produced by Mr Kidd in relation to the 12 offences which were before the magistrates were sufficient to raise a prima facie case of guilty knowledge and, therefore, the magistrates were wrong, even on the evidence they did hear, in concluding that there was no case to answer.

Justice Taylor expressed some surprise that the magistrates reached the conclusion which they did. He did not think it would be right to say that they had erred in coming to that conclusion on the evidence. For one thing, the court had not had that evidence, in detail, before them. They did not know what Mr Kidd said precisely about it or what they would have seen if they had had the documents before them. In those circumstances it would, in his judgment, be wrong to conclude that the magistrates were inevitably bound to say that the respondents had a case to answer in respect of these offences requiring, as they did, guilty knowledge. He therefore answered this question in the negative.

Although he found that the magistrates were wrong to have excluded the evidence as they did, he did not think this was a case in which the appeal could succeed.

CASE 7: "ROADS OPEN TO THE PUBLIC" FOR THE PURPOSES OF THE DRIVERS' HOURS AND TACHOGRAPH REGULATIONS ARE ROADS TO WHICH THE PUBLIC HAVE ACCESS

DPP v Cargo Handling Ltd (2 December 1991)

The Queen's Bench Divisional Court ruled that "roads open to the public" under Council Regulation (EEC) No. 3821/85, of 20 December 1985 on recording equipment in road transport, does not mean "roads maintainable and manageable at public expense" but means "roads to which the public have access".

The Court allowed an appeal by the Director of Public Prosecutions (DPP) against a decision of the Kingston upon Thames magistrates dismissing a charge against the defendant company of using a non-calibrated tachograph in a goods vehicle on a road to which the tachograph regulations applied.

Giving judgment, Lord Justice Leggatt said that under Article 3(1) of Regulation No. 3821/85 the tachograph provisions applied if the vehicle in question was used for the carriage of passengers or goods by road. "Carriage by road" was defined in Article 1 of Regulation No. 3820/85, of 20 December 1985 on the harmonisation of drivers' hours as "any journey made on roads open to the public or a vehicle whether laden or not".

The two roads in question, Shoreham Road West and Southern Perimeter Road, were at Heathrow Airport and were owned by the British Airports Authority (BAA). They were not maintained or managed at public expense and were the responsibility of the BAA. The respondent company was engaged in the conveyance of cargo in bonded freight operations. The magistrates found that the public, as well as passengers, used the premises along the roads. There were no additional physical obstructions to pedestrians. There was a road traffic order which prohibited through traffic.

The magistrates concluded that the words "open to the public" in Article 1 of Regulation No. 3820/85 meant "roads maintainable and manageable at public expense" and that the roads in question were not such roads. They also found that those roads were not roads to which the general public had access, because they were limited to specific classes of persons who were there for limited purposes. They therefore dismissed the charge against the respondent company.

The evidence was that the area of Shoreham Road West was within a Customs controlled area. People going there were there on business. There was a bank, a bar and a restaurant, a hamburger stall and a bus route with bus stops. They were used almost exclusively by airport workers and others who were there on business. The other buildings were all cargo sheds. Through traffic was negligible. There were no physical obstructions to pedestrians in that road.

On the other road there was a petrol station and several bus routes with bus stops. The public as well as passengers were invited to shop at the terminals and use the restaurants and banks. There were hotels adjacent to the perimeter roads. There was also a chemist open until 22.00 hours every night. Sightseers were not allowed on the Southern Perimeter Road, but facilities existed for them at the terminals. There were no signs to indicate that the road traffic enactments did not apply. There was an order under the Road Traffic Regulation Act 1984 that prohibited people from driving straight through the airport, using it as a shortcut, but that prohibition did not prevent sightseers from being in the airport provided they obeyed waiting and loading restrictions, and the indication given by double yellow lines, which have as much force there as elsewhere in England and Wales. Thousands of cars, heavy goods vehicles and passenger carrying vehicles entered and left the airport every day. Many millions of people per annum used those roads.

Photographs had been produced to the magistrates showing that the airport was surrounded by a seven foot high wire fence and that there did not now appear to be unrestricted entry. There were eight main entrances, including the tunnel. All the road signs were at entrances where the public would not have access and there were no road signs in the centre of the airport.

What is a "road open to the public"?

It was argued before the Court that: first, the phrase "open to the public" meant roads maintainable at public expense; and second, if that was wrong, it meant roads to which the public had access, and the magistrates were entitled to find that the general public did not have such access. It was submitted that the purpose of the drivers' hours legislation was to protect the public where drivers of heavy goods vehicles were liable to suffer from fatigue. The mischief aimed at was driving long distances which would, accordingly, involve driving on what might be termed public roads or, more accurately, roads maintainable at the public expense. It was submitted that if the legislature had intended that the words should mean "roads to which the public have access", it would have said so.

With regard to that last point, it seemed that the fact that the legislation in question was European legislation sufficiently explained any difference in the actual phraseology of the article.

The phrase "roads open to the public" did not mean, as a matter of English, "roads maintainable and manageable at the public expense", it meant "roads to which the public have access". Notwithstanding what was said to be the mischief aimed at, there was no way in which the consideration that roads were maintainable at the public expense could be introduced into the definition in question.

Regarding the second argument, it was said that, in relation to the Southern Perimeter Road, it was an offence to use it or any other part of the airport as a shortcut. It was also submitted that only those who had a legitimate interest in attending the airport used the road. Use of the road must, therefore, be taken to be confined to that limited category of person who would be using it in the ordinary course for the particular purpose that that person might have in mind.

In construing the phrase "roads open to the public", familiar cases such as *Harrison v Hill* (1932) had to be looked at. In that case Lord Clyde said:

> *I think also that, when the statute speaks of the public having 'access' to the road, what is meant is neither (at the one extreme) that the public has a positive right of its own to access, nor (at the other extreme) that there exists no physical obstruction, or greater or less impenetrability, against physical access by the public; but that the public actually and legally enjoys access to it. It is, I think, a certain state of use or possession that is pointed to. There must be, as a matter of fact, walking or driving by the public on the road, and such walking or driving must be permitted or allowed, either expressly or implicitly, by the person or persons to whom the road belongs.*

In the same case Lord Sands said:

> *In my view, any road may be regarded as a road to which the public have access upon which members of the public are to be found who have not obtained access whether by overcoming a physical obstruction or in defiance of prohibition express or implied.*

A somewhat different test was proposed by the Lord Chief Justice of Northern Ireland, Lord MacDermott, in *Montgomery v Loney* (1959).

Lord MacDermott said:

> Those who are allowed to enter private property, not as members of the public, but for reasons which are in some way personal to the individuals admitted, will not be regarded as the general public or a substantial section thereof, and their admission will not constitute the giving of access to the public for the purposes of the definition.

Having appraised those observations and taken account of the language used in relation to places of public entertainment, Mr Justice Simon Brown, in *DPP v Vivier* (1992), said in relation to the camp site which was the subject of that case:

> Turning now to the facts of the present appeal, we conclude that there was similarly no sufficient segregation or selection of the caravanners and campers passing through the control system at Unity Farm to cause them to cease to be members of the general public to become instead a special class.

After further considering the circumstances of that case, the Judge concluded by saying:

> It follows that in our judgment the justices here were not entitled, as a matter of law, to reach the conclusion that the users of this park constituted a special class distinct from members of the general public. On the contrary, applying to the facts found, what we believe to be the correct approach of law, is they had no alternative but to find that the general public does indeed have access to the park.

That last paragraph seemed to Lord Justice Leggatt to apply here, substituting "airport" for "park". It could be seen that the roads in question were subject to various restrictions and that shortcuts through the airport were not allowed. On the other hand, thousands of vehicles of all kinds and millions of people used those roads every year. The magistrates, nevertheless, found that access to them was limited to specific classes of persons there for limited purposes, without saying how it was limited and without identifying or defining either the classes or the purposes, except to assert that Shoreham Road West and the shops in the locality were used by people who were there on business.

Since the airport was evidently open to sightseers, that appeared to be a perverse finding. But, even if it were correct, the fact that visitors were there on business did not appear to Lord Justice Leggart to mean they were not members of the public. It was difficult to see how else they could be described generically. Visitors to the airport were from the unselected general public. They had nothing in common except that they went to the airport for various reasons personal to them.

The airport was in no sense a private place except that it was owned and its roads were maintained by the BAA. There were no barriers or obstructions at its entrances by means of which access might be denied to visitors who did not even have to pay to gain admission. It might, indeed, be thought unfortunate if those who drove 3.5 ton vans about the airport were exempted from regulations made for the protection of the public. In his judgment they were not.

There was a certain irony in the fact that, as appeared from the evidence, at every entrance to the airport was a notice which said: "No entry except for access". That concisely expressed what in relation to those roads the public and their vehicles had.

CASE 8: TIMING DRIVERS' WORK AND REST PERIODS

Kelly v Schulman (28 April 1988)

The Queen's Bench Divisional Court ruled that in calculating when the weekly rest period was due, the term "day" in Article 6(1) of Council Regulation (EEC) No. 3820/85, of 20 December 1985 on the harmonisation of certain social legislation in relation to road transport, meant successive periods of 24 hours beginning with the driver's resumption of driving after his or her weekly rest period. It also ruled that every driver had to have a weekly rest period, as defined in Article 8 of Regulation No. 3820/85, once in every week, that is the period between midnight on Sunday and midnight on the following Sunday, and that in certain circumstances the weekly rest period fell to be taken earlier. Thus:

(a) any driver who, in the course of six consecutive driving periods since his or her last weekly rest, had driven in the aggregate not less than the maximum number of hours permitted by the Regulations in six such periods had to begin a weekly rest immediately on the conclusion of the sixth period, but

(b) any such driver who in those six driving periods had driven for an aggregate of less than the maximum number of hours permitted by the Regulations could postpone the commencement of his or her weekly rest period until the end of the sixth day and drive during the period of postponement provided that he or she did not by so doing increase the aggregate of the hours driven since his or her last weekly rest to a figure exceeding the maximum number of hours permitted by the Regulations in six consecutive daily driving periods.

The Court allowed an appeal by Patrick Joseph Kelly against his conviction by the Bradford, West Yorkshire, magistrates on an offence of failing to have 45 consecutive hours of rest after six daily driving periods.

Giving judgment, Mr Justice Hutchison said that Article 6(1) of Regulation No. 3820/85 provided:

> *The daily driving period between any two daily rest periods or between a daily rest period and a weekly rest period, called 'daily driving period', shall not exceed nine hours. It may be extended twice in any one week to 10 hours.*

A driver must, after no more than six daily driving periods, take a weekly rest period as defined in Article 8(3).

The weekly rest period may be postponed until the end of the sixth day if the total driving time over the six days does not exceed the maximum corresponding to six daily driving period.

Article 8 of Regulation No. 3820/85 provided:

- In each period of 24 hours, the driver shall have a daily rest period of at least 11 consecutive hours, which may be reduced to a minimum of nine consecutive hours not more than three times in any one week, on condition that an equivalent period of rest be granted as compensation before the end of the following week.
- In the course of each week, one of the rest periods referred to in paragraphs 1 and 2 shall be extended, by way of weekly rest, to a total of 45 consecutive hours. This rest period may be reduced to a minimum of 36 consecutive hours if taken at the place where the vehicle is normally based or where the driver is based, or to a minimum of 24 consecutive hours if taken elsewhere. Each reduction shall be compensated by an equivalent rest taken en bloc before the end of the third week following the week in question.
- A weekly rest period which begins in one week and continues into the following week may be attached to either of these weeks.

It seemed that the key to understanding the interaction between Articles 6 and 8 was to appreciate that, whereas restrictions in daily driving were expressed in terms of maximum length of driving periods between daily rests, the requirements as to daily rests were expressed in terms of minimum daily rest periods in 24 hours.

Mr Kelly began the particular sequence of work and rest periods on Sunday 4 January 1987, at 15.15 hours. From then until 13.00 hours on Saturday 10 January he worked and rested but all the rest periods were of less than 24 hours' duration.

The magistrates concluded that the term day in Regulation No. 3820/85 meant any 24-hour period commencing at midnight. It followed, if they were correct, that the first day of the period ended at 24.00 on that Sunday, and the sixth day at 24.00 on Friday 9 January. They found that Mr Kelly's sixth daily driving period ended on 10 January at 00.50 and that he thereupon became obliged to take a minimum rest period. Accordingly, they held that by resuming work and driving at 08.45 on 10 January he broke his rest period.

Justice Hutchison considered that the magistrates were wrong in their conclusion. In his view, a day was any period of 24 hours beginning with the resumption of driving after the last weekly rest period. The magistrates had justified their conclusion by reference to the definition of "week" in Article 1 of Regulation No. 3820/85, defined as the period between 00.00 on Monday and 24.00 on Sunday, but he found no support for their view in that definition.

The fact that the Regulation was dealing with an activity which proceeded by day and night militated in favour of a rolling day construction: any successive 24-hour period beginning when the driver resumed driving after a weekly rest period.

The decisive consideration in reaching that conclusion was to be found in the words of Article 6(1) of Regulation No. 3820/85, which stated that: "If the total driving time over the six days does not exceed the maximum corresponding to six daily driving periods".

The qualification to the basic restriction was contemplating a situation when six daily driving periods had taken place in less than six days, and was defining circumstances in which the weekly rest period could be postponed until the end of the sixth day. What possible logic was there in such a provision?

Justice Hutchison drew the following conclusions.

1. The term day in Article 6(1) of Regulation No. 3820/85 meant successive periods of 24 hours beginning with the driver's resumption of driving after his or her weekly rest period.
2. Every driver had to have a weekly rest period, as defined in Article 8 of the Regulation, once in every week, that is, the period between midnight on Sunday and midnight on the following Sunday.
3. In certain circumstances the weekly rest period fell to be taken earlier. Thus:
    (a) any driver who, in the course of six consecutive driving periods since his or her last weekly rest, had driven in the aggregate not less than the maximum number of hours permitted by the Regulations in six such periods had to begin a weekly rest immediately on the conclusion of the sixth period, but
    (b) any such driver who in those six driving periods had driven for an aggregate of less than the maximum number of hours permitted by the Regulations could postpone the commencement of his or her weekly rest period until the end of the sixth day and drive during the period of postponement provided that he or she did not by so doing increase the aggregate of the hours driven since his or her last weekly rest to a figure exceeding the maximum number of hours permitted by the Regulations in six consecutive daily driving periods.

CASE 9: WILFUL IGNORANCE IS NOT "CAUSING AN OFFENCE"

Redhead Freight Ltd v Schulman (28 April 1988)

The Queen's Bench Divisional Court ruled that a company which shut its eyes to the fact that an employee was not filling in his tachograph records could not be said to have caused the employee not to use the tachograph, contrary to s.97(1) of the Transport Act 1968.

The Court allowed an appeal by Redhead Freight Ltd against the decision of the Bradford, West Yorkshire, magistrates who had convicted the company of two offences of causing one of its employees to use a goods vehicle when the tachograph was not being used in accordance with the regulations.

Giving judgment, Lord Justice Woolf said that s.97 of the Transport Act 1968 provided:

1. ...no driver shall drive a vehicle...unless (a) there is installed in the vehicle in the prescribed place and manner equipment for recording information as to the use of the vehicle...

4. Any person who —
   (a) contravenes subsection (1) of this section; or
   (b) being the employer of any other person, or a person to whose orders any other person is subject, causes or permits that other person to contravene that subsection...shall be liable...to a fine

There was no dispute from the evidence that the company knew, or at least deliberately shut its eyes through its transport manager to the fact, that one of its employees was not filling in the tachograph records except on isolated occasions.

However, the very fact that on one occasion the driver did not commit the offence emphasised the problem from the prosecution's point of view. It was not a situation where the inevitable consequence of sending out that driver was that the tachograph record would not be filled out.

Although there was acquiescence in the record-keeping which could amount to permission, it fell short of a positive mandate or any other sufficient act required for the offence as charged.

CASE 10: PERMITTING DRIVERS' HOURS OFFENCES

Light v DPP (13 May 1994)

The Queen's Bench Divisional Court ruled that a transport manager permitted offences by drivers by not responding positively to their continued offending. It could not be said that he had done all he could to discourage breaches of the regulations by continuing to issue the same warnings in standard form time and again despite the frequency of the continuing contraventions. At the very least it was incumbent upon him to ensure that the warnings were carried to the next logical stage, namely disciplinary action.

The Court dismissed an appeal by Kevin Light against the decision of the Middleton, North Manchester, magistrates convicting him of 12 offences of permitting drivers to breach the drivers' hours and tachograph regulations.

Giving judgment, Lord Justice Simon Brown said that the summonses had been issued pursuant to s.96(11A) of the Transport Act 1968, which stated that:

> *Where, in the case of a driver of a motor vehicle, there is in Great Britain a contravention of any requirement of the applicable Community rules as to period of driving or distance driven, or periods on and off duty, then the offender and any other person (being the offender's employer or a person to whose orders the offender was subject) who caused or permitted the contravention shall be liable on summary conviction to a fine*

The applicable Community rules were Articles 6(1) and 7(1) of Council Regulation (EEC) No. 3820/85, of 20 December 1985 on the harmonisation of certain social legislation in relation to road transport. The drivers concerned had contravened the requirements of those articles: in some instances they had driven in excess of the maximum permitted number of hours allowed for the day, contrary to Article 6(1); and in other instances they had driven for more than 4½ hours without observing the necessary 45 minute break, contrary to Article 7(1).

All 12 offences were alleged to have occurred between 19 June and 13 July 1992. The defendant was at the time the transport manager of Airspeed Cargo (London) Ltd, trading as Groundspeed, the company which employed the goods vehicle drivers concerned. He had worked in the transport industry since 1974 and held a Certificate of Professional Competence.

The prosecution case against the defendant was that within the terms of s.96(11A) of the Transport Act 1968 he was "a person to whose orders the offender [the driver] was subject" and that he permitted the various contraventions.

Among the facts found by the magistrates were these. As transport manager the defendant was responsible for ascertaining whether the company's drivers understood the law relating to tachographs and, if necessary, arranging for instruction to be given with regard to their use. He was also responsible for collecting tachograph charts for all the company's drivers on a weekly basis. Every four or six weeks those charts were taken for analysis to a company called Tachocard. The defendant would usually be aware of the results of that analysis within 7–10 days. He inspected all the results. If any breaches of the Regulations were revealed, he interviewed the driver in question and both he and the driver would then sign the analysis sheet, which would be regarded as a warning letter to the driver. Those documents were in standard form and read:

> Dear Mr [driver's name],
>
> Following the examination of your tachograph charts, over the period given below, the following faults and infringements were noted. It is a legal requirement that these points are brought to your attention.

There then followed details of all the various infringements, with their date and the circumstances. The letter continued:

> You should be aware that repeated breaches of driving regulations will render you liable to disciplinary action. If there are any queries regarding the above, please contact your transport manager.
> Report issued by...
> Report received by...

In each instance the defendant at that point signed his name and there followed in each case the driver's signature.

After one of the company's vehicles had been stopped on 24 July 1992, police officers obtained tachograph charts for all the company's drivers. The following facts emerged: 68 tachograph charts relating to the driver Fred Bissett were found to reveal 35 offences; 41 charts relating to the driver Malcolm Chandler revealed 57 offences; 55 charts relating to the driver Fabian Jones revealed 35 offences; and 57 charts relating to the driver James Mitchell revealed 33 offences. Those were the four drivers whose contraventions of Regulation No. 3820/85 the defendant was alleged by the various summonses to have permitted. The offences seemed to start around April

DRIVERS' HOURS AND TACHOGRAPHS

1992, at a time when the company changed its procedures with regard to the "booking in" of deliveries. Before the offences alleged by the summonses, the defendant was aware that offences had been committed by two of the four named drivers.

The prosecution case was that, as a result of the system operated, the defendant acquired the requisite knowledge of repeated contraventions of the Regulation. It was submitted that the number of offences and the period of time over which they occurred raised the inference that the defendant had "turned a blind eye to them" and had thereby permitted them.

On the defendant's behalf it was argued that he had correctly followed the company's checking procedures and properly brought to the drivers' attention their breaches of the Regulation, warning them that "repeated breaches of the driving regulations will render you liable to disciplinary action".

There was no evidence that the defendant could undertake any further disciplinary action beyond the issuing of such warnings. Therefore, rather than turning a blind eye to the breaches, the inference was that the defendant had done all that he could to prevent their repetition.

The magistrates' conclusions were stated as follows.

> *The justices accepted that the offence of permitting was not an absolute offence, nor could it be committed only by virtue of the negligence of the defendant. The prosecutor must prove the defendant had the requisite 'knowledge'. The justices found that the occurrence of the irregularities was capable of providing a foundation for inferring that a person in effective control of the drivers in fact had knowledge or means of knowledge when the irregularities occurred. In view of the findings with regard to the defendant's system of checking the tachograph charts together with the defendant's knowledge of previous offences by the drivers, the justices found that this raised a very strong inference that the defendant had the requisite 'knowledge' or had 'turned a blind eye' to the offending of the drivers. The justices were further confirmed in this opinion by the number of offences the drivers committed and the period over which they occurred.*

The justices then made plain that they had applied the criminal standard of proof.

Did the transport manager permit the offences?

The question posed for the opinion of the Court was simply this: were the justices wrong in law in finding there was sufficient evidence to prove that the defendant had permitted the said offences?

What the defence argument really amounted to was that the defendant did all he could to discourage drivers from breaching the Regulation. His powers went no further than to warn them, and he did precisely as the company's procedures required him to do. Was that sufficient? More particularly, were the magistrates bound to regard it as sufficient? Lord Justice Simon Brown said he could not think so. With the best will in the world it seemed to him impossible to contend that the defendant could do no more than on the face of it he did, namely to content himself with issuing the same warnings in standard form time and again despite the frequency of the continuing contraventions.

At the very least it was surely incumbent upon him, as transport manager, to carry the warnings to the next logical stage, ie disciplinary action, and if not, then surely it was his clear duty to bring the situation to the attention of whoever it was, senior to him in the company hierarchy, who could take the threatened disciplinary action. Why warn a driver of a liability to disciplinary action unless there was in force a system for bringing such repeated breaches to the attention of those who should then take it? The defendant's duty as transport manager responsible for issuing the warnings must surely have gone at least that far. It was for him in evidence to indicate that he took such steps, and it would appear, from the absence of any finding to that effect, that he failed to do so.

In Lord Justice Simon Brown's judgment, that provided an ample basis upon which the magistrates were entitled to reach the conclusion they came to. Here was somebody in a position to carry disciplinary proceedings further but who, on the face of the evidence, chose not to do so. That entitled the magistrates to conclude that the defendant, by not responding more positively to the continued offending on the part of the drivers, did indeed permit such contraventions as thereafter occurred.

Agreeing, Mr Justice Buckley said that in his judgment Lord Justice Simon Brown had amply demonstrated that there was a very obvious inference to be drawn that the defendant was in a position to instigate disciplinary procedure or, at the very least, take or instigate some action against persistently offending drivers. He did not do so and that raised a clear case against him of "permitting". Had he given evidence to rebut that case, to the effect that he had taken action and that the company, for its own commercial ends perhaps, had refused to implement it, that might very well have provided him with some defence. The Court understood that he did not give evidence to that effect.

The magistrates were therefore fully entitled, for the reasons they gave, to reach the conclusion that they did.

CASE 11: "PERMISSIBLE MAXIMUM WEIGHT" MEANS "GROSS WEIGHT OF VEHICLE AND TRAILER"

Small v DPP (15 March 1994)

The Queen's Bench Divisional Court ruled that where a vehicle was required by the EC Regulations to have a tachograph installed, the expression "permissible maximum weight" referred to the maximum gross weight of the vehicle and trailer and not to their maximum train weight.

The Court allowed an appeal by Peter Small, trading as Ascane Imports, against a decision of the Pontefract magistrates convicting him of an offence under s.97(1)(a) of the Transport Act 1968 of using a motor van and single-axle trailer on a road without having a tachograph fitted as required by Council Regulation (EEC) No. 3821/85, of 20 December 1985 on recording equipment in road transport.

Giving judgment, Mr Justice Wright said that s.97 applied to vehicles and trailers over 3.5 tonnes. There was an exception for vehicles below that weight in accordance with Article 4 of Council Regulation (EEC) No. 3820/85, of 20 December 1985 on the harmonisation of certain social legislation in relation to road transport, which was incorporated in Regulation No. 3821/85.

The determining factor was the permissible maximum weight of the vehicle as expressed in Article 1 of Regulation No. 3820/85. The expression related to an aggregate of the maximum gross weight marked on the van and of the maximum gross weight marked on the trailer in actual use, and not to the total weight of the vehicle and trailer which it might be capable of drawing.

The maximum train weight of a vehicle and trailer was defined separately in s.108 of the Road Traffic Act 1988.

In his judgment the appeal must succeed.

COURT OF APPEAL (CRIMINAL DIVISION)

CASE 12: DRIVERS WHO FALSIFY TACHOGRAPH RECORDS ABROAD AND THEN PRODUCE THEM ARE GUILTY OF AN OFFENCE UNDER THE FORGERY AND COUNTERFEITING ACT 1981

Regina v Anthony Colin Osman, Richard Mills and Robert Chalker (9 December 1993)

The Court of Appeal dismissed appeals by the three defendants against their convictions on offences brought under the Forgery and Counterfeiting Act 1981 relating to the falsification of tachograph records.

Giving judgment, Lord Justice Kennedy said that following a ruling by a Crown Court judge, each of the defendants had pleaded guilty at Winchester Crown Court to offences of using a false instrument, namely a tachograph chart, which they knew or believed to be false, with the intention of inducing somebody to accept the same as genuine. They subsequently were given leave to appeal against those convictions.

The appellants were long-distance lorry drivers employed by Bulldog Transport and they frequently drove in mainland Europe. If they could overcome the restrictions as to the hours and distances to be driven by such drivers, and the requirement to keep their tachograph running, they could work longer hours and earn more money, and their employers would have greater use from their employees and vehicles and thus be more competitive.

The prosecution case was that the three appellants had falsified their tachograph records and in due course handed over the false tachograph charts to their employer, who might or might not have known at that time that the charts were false. That reservation was made because when in late 1990 inspectors went to Bulldog Transport and sought production of the charts, the employer apparently attempted to hide or dispose of them. However, a number were traced and examined, and so the three appellants faced a number of counts each relating to a different period between June and November 1990.

When the matter came before Judge Starforth-Hill at Winchester Crown Court on 12 October 1990, before the arraignment (trial), the judge was persuaded that there was a point of law which, if decided in favour of the defence, would be determinative of the case. This concerned whether, assuming the facts to be as set out in the prosecution statements, an assumption which was not likely it appeared to be seriously in dispute, it would be open to a jury properly directed to convict. Counsel agreed that the matter should be argued before the arraignment, and so it was. The judge then gave his ruling and the appellants changed their pleas.

The Court of Appeal considered that the procedure adopted was incorrect. This view was held because of the decision of the Court in the case of *Regina v Jones and others* (1974) where Lord Widgery said:

> Upon a motion to quash a count made before arraignment the judge gives his ruling upon the form and matter on the face of the indictment. Only in one circumstance can the judge look beyond the indictment to the depositions or statements. That is when the motion to quash is on the ground that the offence is not disclosed by the depositions or statements, and there has been no committal for trial of that offence.

(See Lord Chief Justice Goddard in *Chairman of London County Sessions ex parte Downes* (1953), cited with approval by Lord Morris of Borth-y-Gest in *Connelly v DPP* (1963).)

Accordingly, it seemed to them that when the possibility of a submission of the type which was being made to Judge Starforth-Hill arose, the judge should have rejected it on the basis that the submission was not being made at the correct time. The jury should have been selected, the accused should have been arraigned, the matter should then have gone to the close of the prosecution case, and at that stage, if thought appropriate, this submission could then have been made. The reason for following that course was relatively obvious, namely if that sort of submission was to be made, the appropriate time and place to make it would have been before the magistrates at the committal. Apparently no submission was then made, or if it was made it was rejected.

Turning to the substance of the submission itself, these charges were brought under s.3 of the Forgery and Counterfeiting Act 1981, which read as follows.

> It is an offence for a person to use an instrument which is and which he knows and believes to be false with the intention of inducing somebody

to accept it as genuine, and by reason of so accepting it to do or not to do some act to his own or any other person's prejudice.

Clearly, therefore, the criminal act was the using of the instrument with the requisite intent.

There had to be a double intent (see *Regina v Tobierre* (1985)): there had to be an intention both to induce someone to accept the instrument as genuine and that other person should act or choose not to act to his or her own or someone else's prejudice.

Unquestionably it would seem that Mr Osman used the tachograph chart when he passed it to his employer, if the evidence showed that he did pass it to his employer. The Court of Appeal made that reservation because that was precisely the sort of matter which they would expect to be covered by evidence during the course of the prosecution case. If he passed it to his employer and the employer was also aware of the falseness of the document, because it was apparently accepted that Mr Osman was well aware that the document itself was false, then it seemed to them the intention on the part of the driver was to induce somebody in the shape of an inspector, if an inspector ever came to look at it, to accept that tachograph chart as genuine, and by reason of so accepting it to do or not to do some act to his own or any other person's prejudice within the meaning of that phrase as defined in s.10, subsection 1(c) of the Forgery and Counterfeiting Act 1981.

Alternatively, if the employer were not a party to the arrangement, in that the employer did not know that the tachograph chart was false when it came into his possession, then it would seem on the face of it that the intention on the part of the driver was to induce the employer to accept it as genuine, and by reason of so accepting it, to do or not to do some act to his (the employer's) own prejudice.

Accordingly, on the face of it, it would seem that even if it were possible to make the submission at the time when it was made, it was a submission that ought to have been rejected. In those circumstances it seemed that although the matter did not proceed in the proper way, they could say that no injustice had been done. The fact was that the application should have been refused and the submission should have been rejected; once the submission was in fact rejected these appellants pleaded. Accordingly this appeal must be dismissed.

OPERATORS' LICENSING

HIGH COURT OF JUSTICE (QUEEN'S BENCH DIVISION)

CASE 13: OPERATOR'S LICENSING EXEMPTION FOR EMERGENCY VEHICLES

Wing v TD & C Kelly Ltd (2 December 1996)

The Queen's Bench Divisional Court ruled that owners of a vehicle kept for use in an emergency are only exempt from the need to obtain an operator's licence if they are a business for the supply of water, gas, electricity or telephone services.

The Court allowed an appeal by Elaine Wing, on behalf of the Department of Transport Vehicle Inspectorate, against a decision of the Prestatyn magistrates to acquit the company TD & C Kelly Ltd of an offence of unlawfully using a goods vehicle, contrary to s.60 of the Transport Act 1968.

Giving judgment, Mr Justice Collins said that the magistrates had found that the company's vehicle was exempt from the need to obtain an operator's licence for its use as an emergency vehicle because it fell within the definition in paragraph 27 of schedule 5, Part I to the Goods Vehicles (Operators Licences, Qualifications and Fees) Regulations 1984. That definition was now enacted in paragraph 26 of schedule 3, Part I to the Goods Vehicles (Licensing of Operators) Regulations 1995. It provided an exemption for "a vehicle held ready for use in an emergency by an undertaking for the supply of water, gas, electricity or telephone services".

It had been argued on behalf of the company that although the vehicle was not attending an emergency, it was ready so to do. It was not necessary that the vehicle was solely ready for such use. All that was necessary was that it was available for use in an emergency.

OPERATORS' LICENSING

Mr Justice Collins considered that the definition could not be read completely literally because any vehicle being used, when en route, was not being "held". The paragraph was descriptive of the type of vehicle which might broadly be termed an emergency vehicle.

Even if the vehicle was ready for use in an emergency, the owners had to be an undertaking for the supply of relevant services. The company was not such an undertaking.

In his judgment, the appeal should be allowed.

OVERLOADING

HIGH COURT OF JUSTICE (QUEEN'S BENCH DIVISION)

CASE 14: SEPARATE OFFENCES CREATED FOR EACH PERMITTED WEIGHT EXCEEDED

Travel-Gas (Midlands) Ltd v Frank Reynolds and others and J H Myers Ltd v Licensing Authority for the North East Traffic Area (22 June 1988)

The Queen's Bench Divisional Court ruled that regulation 80(1)(a) and (b) of the Road Vehicles (Construction and Use) Regulations 1986 created separate offences for each permitted weight exceeded.

The Court dismissed appeals by Travel-Gas (Midlands) Ltd and J H Myers Ltd and others against their convictions for offences of overloading.

Giving judgment, Mr Justice MacPherson said that on 1 May 1987 an information (accusation) was laid against Travel-Gas saying that it had both used a vehicle on a road in Dartmouth Middleway when the gross weight exceeded the permitted plated weight and used the same vehicle when the permitted rear axle weight was exceeded. Both offences were said to be contrary to regulation 80 of the Road Vehicles (Construction and Use) Regulations 1986. The company pleaded guilty to the first of the offences, namely the gross weight offence. There was then argument over whether it was correct in law for the magistrates to proceed on the second information relating to the rear axle weight. It was argued by the defence that the 1986 Regulations were worded differently from the previous Regulations. The prosecution maintained that the 1986 Regulations were simply a repeat in different words of the earlier Regulations. The *J H Myers and others* case was very similar, and there was really no material difference between the two cases.

The magistrates ruled that the prosecutor could proceed on more than one information.

Background to the Regulations

There had been three separate sets of Regulations, first those of 1973, second those of 1978 and last those of 1986. It was apparent, on looking at those Regulations, that they had shortened and evolved. All that had happened was that the legislators, or those considering the drafting of the Regulations, had sought to compress the matters set out in the earlier Regulations into a new form in the 1986 Regulations.

Regulation 80(1) read:

> Subject to paragraph (2), no person shall use, or cause or permit to be used, on a road a vehicle
>
> (a) fitted with a plate in accordance with Regulation 66, but for which no plating certificate has been issued, if any of the weights shown on the plate is exceeded;
>
> (b) for which a plating certificate has been issued, if any of the weights shown in column (2) of the plating certificate is exceeded

The Court was told that a different vice was aimed at in respect of the two separate restrictions. The gross weight restriction was aimed, primarily, at braking and other vices, and difficulties of management of the vehicle on the road. The axle weight restriction, while perhaps also aiming at that, had enshrined in it an attack upon those who used vehicles with overweight single axles, since they might cause excessive damage to the road surface and to bridges.

Can separate cases be brought for each permitted weight exceeded?

The Court first had to consider simply whether, in law, it was allowable to issue two informations, one in respect of gross weight and another in respect of axle weight.

In the opinion of Justice MacPherson, the 1986 Regulations did no more than enshrine what was set out in the earlier regulations. If this were not so, the regulation should have been phrased "if any one of the weights shown on the plate is exceeded". Where the wording was "if any of the weights shown on the plate is exceeded", the prosecuting authority was correct to look to see whether the gross weight had been exceeded and whether any of the individual weights in respect of up to six axles which might be borne on a vehicle had individually been exceeded.

In Justice MacPherson's judgment that was really the end of the case. It was not a case where duplicity arose. The law as to duplicity was aimed at accused persons who were put into difficulty by a double allegation and did not really know what case they had to meet. Here the question was whether one or more offences was actually enshrined in the Regulations themselves.

In his judgment, in law each prosecuting authority was entitled, if there was a gross overweight and an axle overweight or axle overweights, to bring separate informations.

In response to the argument that it was oppressive to bring more than one information, he said that if a prosecuting authority found there was overweight and exactly even distribution over the axles, there might be cases in which it was fairer and better that only one information should be laid. But the Court was not concerned with a question of policy and did not know what might lie behind a decision that separate informations should be brought.

Furthermore, to bring separate informations laid before the accused person or company the fact that there had been overweight generally, and in respect of one, two or three axles. When the matter came to court different considerations might arise, but again the matter was one for the prosecuting authority's discretion.

If there was a plea of guilty to an overall overweight information and there was really nothing at all added by the other information or informations in respect of separate axles, it might be fair and wise simply to accept the plea on the gross weight information because it could be said to be oppressive to proceed further and put before the magistrates the possibility of £4000 in fines, or more, if there were more than one individual axle overweight, when £2000 was the maximum for the gross overweight of the vehicle. But in his judgment, that must be a matter for the discretion of the prosecution.

In law, however, there was nothing to stop a prosecuting authority going ahead on both summonses, and the magistrates would then no doubt wish to know the facts and the vice which was said to be present in each case, and would assess the penalty which was necessary overall.

He was comforted in this decision by that in *J Theobald (Hounslow) Ltd and another v Stacy* (1979), in which Mr Justice Lloyd referred to the judgment of Lord

Parker in the case of *Regina v Burnham, Bucks Justices ex parte Ansorge* (1959) and said:

> which puts the matter, as it seems to me, at its most favourable from the defendants' point of view: are the facts required to support a conviction in relation to gross weight the very same facts as would be required to support a conviction in relation to axle weights? It seems to me that one only has to ask oneself that question to see that the answer must be 'No'. The offences are not the same offences. The fact that the offences were committed simultaneously is immaterial. Nor, in my judgment, is it material that on the facts of this particular case the defendants could not commit one offence without also committing one or both the others. Any hardship which may result from multiple convictions, where they occur, can, it seems to me, be mitigated when it comes to the question of penalty.

It seemed to him that those words were entirely apt in the two cases which were before the Court.

Agreeing, Lord Justice Watkins said that he would merely add a word or two about the exercise of the prosecutor's discretion in such cases. It was important that the courts were not over-burdened by being called upon to consider unnecessary charges and, likewise, defendants did not have to face unnecessary charges.

In that respect it had been brought to their attention that occasionally, in addition to the transport company which owned the motor vehicle being proceeded against, the driver at the relevant time had also been prosecuted. Whether that duplication of prosecution should take place was obviously a matter which the prosecuting authority was very properly concerned with. But in the exercise of its discretion as to whether or not it was necessary to proceed against both "master" and "servant", the prosecuting authority should bear very much in mind the question whether there was a feature of a particular case which pointed to a special culpability lying upon the driver of the vehicle. If there was not, then it seemed to be wholly unnecessary to proceed against the driver as well as the owner of the vehicle.

With those few observations he sought to emphasise that the exercise of a discretion in the prosecutor really meant what it said: a very careful appraisal of the circumstances in order to see that only those charges which it was absolutely necessary upon the facts to bring were in fact brought.

As to what happened in court during the proceedings, here again Lord Justice Watkins agreed that the prosecuting authority had a discretion as to whether or not to proceed further with outstanding charges when the leading charge had, so to speak, been dealt with by way of a plea of guilty by a defendant.

If what concerned the prosecutor in that event was solely the question of penalty, then unless the seriousness of the leading charge demanded it, in his view the exercise of the discretion should lead the prosecutor against insisting that the justices go on to consider the outstanding charges.

But he well understood that there might be circumstances in which the leading charge was so serious a matter, and the record of the defendant so bad, as to properly cause the prosecutor to invite the justices to consider the outstanding charges so that the punishment might more adequately represent the seriousness of the whole conduct of the defendant than otherwise it would.

CASE 15: REGULATION 80(1) AND (2) DO NOT CREATE SEPARATE OFFENCES

DPP v Marshall and Bell (14 April 1989)

The Queen's Bench Divisional Court ruled that regulation 80(1) and (2) of the Road Vehicles (Construction and Use) Regulations 1986 do not create separate offences.

The Court allowed an appeal by the Director of Public Prosecutions (DPP) against the acquittal of the defendants who had been charged with an axle overloading offence.

Giving judgment, Mr Justice Saville said that the respondents were prosecuted for using a rigid tipper on a road contrary to regulation 80(1)(b).

Regulation 80 (1) read:

> Subject to paragraph (2), no person shall use, or cause or permit to be used, on a road a vehicle:
>
> (a) fitted with a plate in accordance with Regulation 66, but for which no plating certificate has been issued, if any of the weights shown on the plate is exceeded;
>
> (b) for which a plating certificate has been issued, if any of the weights shown in column (2) of the plating certificate is exceeded

Paragraph 2 provided:

> Where any two or more axles are fitted with compensating arrangements in accordance with regulation 23, the sum of the weights shown for them in the plating certificate shall not be exceeded. In a case where the plating certificate has not been issued the sum of the weights referred to shall be that shown for the said axles in the plate fitted in accordance with regulation 66.

Before the magistrates it was argued that since the specific limits on use stipulated in paragraph 1 were made expressly subject to paragraph 2, and since the vehicle was one which fell within the provisions of paragraph 2 because it had compensating axles, the offence alleged, namely use contrary to paragraph 1(b), was one which the defendants had not committed since paragraph 1(b) did not apply to the vehicle in question. It was maintained that the defendants had been charged with the wrong offence.

OVERLOADING

Two things were, to Justice Saville's mind, to be noted. First, the vital words in question were "subject to". Second, the specific prohibition that no person shall use, or cause or be permitted to be used, a vehicle was contained in paragraph 80(1). Looking at those two points together, it seemed to him that the words "subject to" really applied a proviso or qualification to the specific prohibitions set out in paragraph 80(1). The intent, therefore, was that an offence might be committed under paragraph 80(1) in the case of a vehicle fitted with a compensating arrangement. This was because paragraph 1(b) was subject to the qualification in paragraph 2 and was to be read with that qualification; so that a vehicle with a compensating arrangement — the sum of whose weights exceeded that shown in the plating certificate — was a vehicle that contravened paragraph 80(1)(b).

If it had been intended to make the case of vehicles with compensating axle arrangements quite distinct and separate from the prohibition in paragraph 80(1), Justice Saville would have expected to see words stronger that the words "subject to" used, such as "save as provided in" or other words of similar effect. He would also have expected to see a prohibition on use in the second paragraph as well as in the first. As it was, the prohibition on use was in paragraph 1. "Subject to" were words that to his mind imported a qualification rather than an exception. In those circumstances, it seemed to him that the true meaning and effect of regulation 80 was that an offence was created by paragraph 80(1) which in specific circumstances, namely those concerning vehicles fitted with a compensating arrangement, was to be read subject to the qualification imposed by paragraph 2.

OVERLOADING

CASE 16: EVIDENCE THAT COMPUTERISED WEIGHBRIDGES ARE WORKING PROPERLY

East West Transport Ltd v DPP (15 February 1995)

The Queen's Bench Divisional Court ruled that magistrates require evidence that the electronic computer controlling a dynamic axle weighbridge is operating properly before convicting operators and drivers of overloading offences.

The Court allowed appeals by East West Transport Ltd against the company's conviction on three offences of overloading.

Giving judgment, Mr Justice Potts said that it was alleged before the Milton Keynes magistrates that East West Transport Ltd had used an articulated outfit on the M1 motorway when the permitted weight of the first axle, the second axle and the gross weight of the tractor unit were exceeded. The vehicle was stopped by a police officer because the tractor unit looked heavy, and the driver was directed to a dynamic axle weighbridge adjacent to junction 14 on the M1 motorway. The police officer gave evidence as to the manner in which the vehicle was weighed. The original printout of the weighing was produced. Evidence was given by a senior Trading Standards officer that the weighbridge had been checked for accuracy in March and October 1993 and was within accepted tolerances. He also gave evidence that the machine performed a calibration check and a red light flashed if the speed of the vehicle being weighed was too high.

From the evidence of those witnesses, the magistrates were satisfied that the weighbridge was working properly on the relevant occasion. They said that evidence of mechanical devices was acceptable without proof of their accuracy if the court thought fit and the excess weight shown was considerable. Its view was that the printout was produced at the time and was analogous to the printout from a Lion Intoximeter. Therefore, in the absence of evidence that the machine was not functioning properly they were entitled to rely upon the printout.

The printout was produced by a computer. Section 69(1) of the Police and Criminal Evidence Act 1984 provides that in any proceedings a statement in a document produced by a computer shall not be admissible as evidence of any fact stated in it unless it was shown that:

(a) there were no reasonable grounds for believing that the statement was inaccurate because of improper use of the computer

(b) at all material times the computer was operating properly or, if not, that any malfunction would not affect the production of the document or the accuracy of its contents.

In the decision of *House of Lords in Regina v Shepherd* (1993), it was said that that section of the Act was of general application to documents produced by computer and it required anyone who wished to introduce computer evidence to produce evidence that would establish that it was safe to rely on the documents produced by the computer. Such a duty could not be discharged without evidence by applying the presumption that the computer was working correctly.

Justice Potts rejected arguments that the magistrates were entitled to draw the conclusion that the police officer was satisfied that the weighbridge was operating correctly from his evidence as to the manner in which the vehicle was weighed. There had been no finding that he had given evidence as to the reliability of the weighbridge.

Neither did he accept arguments that the Trading Standards officer's evidence (ie that the machine performed a calibration check and that a red light flashed if the speed of the vehicle being weighed was too high) entitled the magistrates to find that the computer was working properly at the material time.

There was no satisfactory evidence that the computer, that is to say the weighbridge, was functioning correctly on the date when the company's vehicle was weighed.

CASE 17: ENTITLED TO RELY UPON CERTIFICATE OF WEIGHT

Cormac Leonard v Vehicle Inspectorate (5 February 1996)

The Queen's Bench Divisional Court ruled that magistrates are entitled to rely upon the Certificate of Weight, and the printout from a dynamic axle weigher, as evidence of the weight recorded by a weighbridge.

The Court dismissed appeals by Cormac Leonard against his conviction on an offence of overloading.

Giving judgment, Mr Justice Blofeld said that evidence was given before the Morley magistrates that the articulated outfit concerned was escorted to a dynamic axle weigher, where it was weighed. The weighing was carried out by a Mr Pollard, who was acting in his capacity as an enforcement officer, in accordance with the Codes of Practice for the weighing of goods vehicles. He found that the weights on the axles exceeded the maximum on the plate by 8.6%. He then received a copy of the computer printout from the weighing machine and endorsed it with the registration number. He then completed a Certificate of Weight in accordance with the codes of practice. He stated that he was familiar with the codes of practice and their contents. He had set up the computer and had checked it before he weighed this particular vehicle, and then carried out appropriate checks in accordance with the codes of practice. While weighing the vehicle, and after weighing it, he had checked that the computer was working properly.

On those facts, the magistrates found that the dynamic axle weigher had been properly used and was working properly.

The appellants argued that there was insufficient evidence that the computer was working accurately for the magistrates to be satisfied as to the figures that were produced by it. The computer printout was information from a computer and s.69(1) of the Police and Criminal Evidence Act 1984 required proof that the computer was reliable. As the Certificate of Weight issued by Mr Pollard was, in part, a copying of the figures on the computer printout, then any criticism that could be made of the computer printout could also be made of the Certificate.

In the House of Lords decision in the case of *Shepherd*, Lord Griffiths said that the reliability of the computer could be proved in two ways: either by calling oral evidence or by tendering a written certificate. But that was a totally different certificate from the one being considered in the present case.

Lord Griffiths had come to the conclusion that the evidence on the facts relating to this particular case was sufficient for the magistrates to draw the inferences that they did. It was clear they had found that Mr Pollard had carried out his work in accordance with the codes of practice which related specifically to the computer. He was satisfied that the evidence by Mr Pollard was itself sufficient in the circumstances of the case.

Section 79(4) of the Road Traffic Act 1988 states:

> A certificate in the prescribed form which:
>
> (a) purports to be signed by an authorised person (within the meaning of Section 78 of this Act)...
>
> (b) states, in relation to a vehicle identified in the certificate, any weight determined in relation to that vehicle on the occasion of it being brought to a weighbridge or other machine in pursuance of a requirement under Section 78(1) of this Act, shall be evidence... of the matter so stated.

The Road Traffic Act 1988 was subsequent to the Police and Criminal Evidence Act 1984. Clearly, on the face of it, those words meant precisely what they said: that the contents of that Certificate shall be evidence of the matter so stated. Consequently, the Certificate by itself would be sufficient evidence, unless the contrary was proved, for the court to act upon.

Justice Griffiths also considered that the computer printout was properly admissible in the proceedings without reference to s.69 of the Police and Criminal Evidence Act 1984. Although the regulations referred to in the Road Traffic Act 1988 were made before the Police and Criminal Evidence Act 1984, s.78 (5) included the words:

> Regulations... above may make provision with respect to... (b) the limits... for the purposes of any provision made by or under this Act or by or under any other enactment relating to motor vehicles or trailers.

That seemed to him to provide an exception to the provisions of s.69 of the Police and Criminal Evidence Act 1984.

Agreeing, Lord Justice Saville said that assuming s.69(1) of the Police and Criminal Evidence Act 1984 was applicable, he was satisfied that there was sufficient evidence to show both proper use of the computer and that the computer was operating properly at the time given by Mr Pollard.

He also agreed that the Certicate of Weight that Mr Pollard prepared was admissible as evidence by virtue of s.79(4) of the Road Traffic Act 1988 and that the computer printout itself was also admissible by virtue of s.78(5) of that Act and regulation 4 of the Weighing of Motor Vehicles (Use of Dynamic Axle Weighing Machines) Regulations 1978.

CASE 18: OWNER DOES NOT "USE" VEHICLE WHEN IT IS DRIVEN BY SELF-EMPLOYED DRIVER

West Yorkshire Trading Standards Service v Lex Vehicle Leasing Ltd (9 February 1995)

The Queen's Bench Divisional Court ruled that a person was the user of a vehicle only if the driver was employed by the owner under a contract of service and at the material time was driving on the employer's business.

The Court dismissed an appeal by West Yorkshire Trading Standards Service against a decision of the Huddersfield magistrates dismissing a charge of overloading brought against Lex Vehicle Leasing Ltd.

Giving judgment, Mr Justice Dyson said that an information (accusation) was laid against the defendant company alleging that it had used a motor vehicle, namely a car transporter, on a road when the maximum permitted weight of the front axle was exceeded. The driver of the motor vehicle referred to, Mr Gordon Sheppard, was convicted of using the transporter at the relevant time with a laden weight on the front axle which exceeded the maximum permitted.

The magistrates found the following facts. The defendant company owned the vehicle and had no reason to believe that their specifications had not been complied with. On 12 February 1993 the vehicle was being driven by Mr Sheppard, who at that time was using the vehicle on the defendant company's business. Mr Sheppard worked for the defendant company under an operating agreement for self-employed drivers: he was classed by the defendant company as "on supply".

Mr Sheppard was paid by the defendant company on a daily basis calculated according to the distance travelled and was entitled to expenses. He paid his own tax and national insurance and employed the services of an accountant to prepare trading accounts for tax purposes.

Jobs were allocated to him as and when they were available. He was not under any obligation to work exclusively for the defendant company. While working for the defendant company, Mr Sheppard drove its vehicles, wore the company uniform and collected and delivered loads from and to specified locations. He decided his route and how to load the transporter and he took breaks at his own discretion. From the time he collected the transporter until he returned it, the transporter was in Mr Sheppard's possession and the defendant company did not control its activities.

OVERLOADING

Before the magistrates, it was argued on behalf of the defendant company that it was not the user of the vehicle because the driver, Mr Sheppard, was not its employee, but was a self-employed contractor. On behalf of the prosecution, it was submitted that Mr Sheppard was, on the facts, an employee of the company and, consequently, his use of the transporter constituted use by the defendant company. Alternatively, it was argued that the transporter was owned by the defendant company and used by Mr Sheppard on its business and under its direction; the defendant company determined the load to be carried so that the defendant company used the transporter on the day in question.

The magistrates decided that the defendant company was not Mr Sheppard's employer and therefore was not using the transporter when he drove it at the material time. The finding that the defendant company was not Mr Sheppard's employer was not being challenged in this appeal.

The appellant made the following submissions. First, it was accepted that there was a line of authority in this type of case to the effect that where an offence was not merely an offence of the user but could also be an offence of causing or permitting the user, a restricted meaning should be given to the word "use". That restricted meaning had involved construing the word "used" as being limited to the driver of the vehicle and to the owner of the vehicle, provided that:

(a) the driver was employed by the owner under a contract of service, in other words he was an employee, and

(b) that at the material time the driver was driving on his employer's business.

Second, it was submitted that in two recent cases a narrow and rigid approach to the meaning of the word use had lapsed and a more flexible approach had been followed, based on common sense.

Third, it was submitted that the magistrates had erred in law in apparently adopting that narrow and rigid approach since they regarded the fact that the defendant company was not Mr Sheppard's employer as decisive and fatal to the prosecution.

Fourth, it was submitted that the magistrates should have adopted the more relaxed approach and decided that the company was using the vehicle at the material time.

Last, it was submitted that, if necessary, the Court should overrule the established line of authority which had been referred to.

On behalf of the defendant company, it was submitted that the Court should, and indeed were obliged to, follow the line of cases which had been referred to, and that the two recent cases relied upon by the appellant were distinguishable.

"Narrow" meaning of the word "use"

The so-called narrow approach to the meaning of the word "use", where it was found in criminal statutes in conjunction with the alternatives of "causes" or "permits", had a long pedigree.

In the case of *Carmichael & Sons Ltd v Cottle* (1971), Lord Chief Justice Parker said:

> It has long been held that, when the offence is not merely an offence of user but can be an offence of causing or permitting the user, a restricted meaning should be given to use. In Windle v Dunning & Son Ltd (1968), this court had to consider a similar matter, and in giving the first judgment in that case I referred in the first instance to Macleod v Penman (1962) in Scotland, where the Lord Justice-General Lord Clyde said: "The presence in the section of the alternatives of causing or permitting the use must limit the scope of what is 'using'. Normally, 'using' is applicable to the actual driver." After having quoted that, I went on... "I entirely agree with that, and in my judgment, 'using' when used in connection with causing and permitting has a restricted meaning. It certainly covers the driver, it may also cover the driver's employer if he, the driver, is about his master's business, but beyond that I find it very difficult to conceive that any other person could be said to be using the vehicle as opposed to causing it to be used."

In *Crawford v Haughton* (1972), a vehicle owned by the defendant was driven by a person named Gaule on a road for the purposes of the defendant's business. The magistrates convicted the defendant of using the vehicle since Gaule was using the vehicle with the defendant's authority and knowledge and for the purposes of his business. In allowing the appeal, the Divisional Court said that the defendant would have been guilty of the alternative charge of permitting the vehicle's use but not of using the vehicle. Lord Chief Justice Widgery referred to *Carmicheal & Sons Ltd v Cottle* (1971) and he said:

> I have not found this a particularly easy case because I find it difficult to accept that, if a man can use a vehicle through the hands of his servant,

> he cannot be said to use it at the hands of someone who at his specific request drives it on a journey at the express orders and with the full knowledge of the owner. No doubt the line must be drawn somewhere, and the judgments of Lord Parker CJ to which I have referred show a tendency to restrict the capacity of persons using in cases where the alternatives of permitting or causing to be used are provided. I have thought for some time that it might be right for us to say in the present case that there is yet another category of user for present purposes, not merely the actual driver or his employer, but someone who by specific and immediate direction causes a vehicle to be driven in the manner in which it was driven in this case. But in the end I have come to the conclusion that it would not be right, in view of the authorities, to strive to extend the meaning of 'use' for the present purposes, and that only confusion may follow in subsequent cases if we endeavour so to do. I have, therefore, come to the conclusion that this is a case on the wrong side of the line as far as the prosecution are concerned.

In *Garrett v Hooper* (1973), the defendant and a person named Towers were partners and joint owners of a vehicle which was partnership property. The vehicle was driven on a road on partnership business by Towers. The defendant was convicted of using the vehicle in contravention of the relevant section and regulations. His appeal was allowed. Having referred to the earlier authorities, Lord Widgery said:

> In *Crawford v Haughton*,... this court recognised the element of illogicality in holding that a man may use a vehicle through his servant but cannot use it through the hands of someone specifically authorised to drive it on the day in question. A similar illogicality will, I fear, follow if we merely follow *Crawford v Haughton* and say that a co-partner does not use a vehicle merely because it is driven by his partner on partnership business. Nevertheless, as I said in *Crawford v Haughton*, the line must be drawn somewhere and it is idle to hope that wherever the line is drawn, decisions on either side of it can be wholly rational. I think that we should follow *Crawford v Haughton* and say that in this case the defendant was not using the partnership vehicle at the relevant time.

In *Howard v G T Jones & Co. Ltd* (1975), the driver was supplied to the defendant company by an employment agency. He drove the defendant company's vehicle on the road on its business. The load was insecure and the defendant company was charged with the use of the vehicle in contravention of the relevant provision of the Road Traffic Act 1972 and the relevant regulation. The defendant company was acquitted on appeal. Lord Widgery referred once again to the line of authorities, saying:

> But up to now although the drawing of the line at that point is not wholly logical, there has been no extension of the categories of persons who can be said to use a vehicle beyond first the driver, and secondly the driver's employer if the driver is working under a contract of service on behalf of the owner of the vehicle. Now the question comes whether in the somewhat different circumstances of this case we ought to say that the present example falls on one side of the line or the other. It is quite clear that the justices in this instance have attempted to follow the authorities to which I have referred; they have applied their minds to the question whether Mr Petts was a servant of the defendants or the agency who paid him his wages, and although they do not say so, there seems to be little doubt that they have considered what one might call the modern criterion to determine whether or not a contract of service exists; they have not actually referred to Global Plant Ltd v Secretary of State for Social Services (1972), but in that case is to be found an up-to-date statement of such criterion. They have evidently approached the matter in that way, whether by reference to that case or not; they have decided that Mr Petts was a servant of the agency, and accordingly have decided that the owners of the vehicle not being the employers of Mr Petts were not using the vehicle for the present purposes. In my judgment we should adhere to the line which was drawn in Crawford v Haughton and the earlier cases. I think, as I said before, that only confusion would be likely to result if we sought to relax the principle which was enunciated in those cases and began to let in as persons who might be driving on behalf of the owner some individuals who were not servants of the owner at all. I think for reasons already given that it would be unfortunate if the categories were extended and accordingly in this case at first sight one ought to adopt the judgment of the justices that Mr Petts was not a servant of the defendants and conclude as they did that the defendants were therefore not using the vehicle.

Thus the line had been clearly and consistently drawn by the Court. A person was a "user" only if he or she was the driver or the owner of the vehicle, but it applied to the owner only if the driver was employed by the owner under a contract of service and was, at the material time, driving on the employer's business. The line had been described variously as not wholly logical and as somewhat artificial, but it had been drawn by the Court after due consideration had been given to those criticisms, to some extent, for pragmatic reasons and to avoid confusion.

Should the Court follow previous cases?

Before turning to the two recent cases, it was necessary to deal with the appellant's submission that the Court should decline to follow that line of cases. That line of cases had not been overruled in either of the two recent cases. It was clear that in limited circumstances the Court could decline to follow a previous decision of the Court.

The approach that was to be adopted was the same as that applied by the Court of Appeal (Criminal Division) when it considered an earlier decision of the Court to have been wrong. The authority for that proposition was *Regina v Manchester Coroner ex parte Tal* (1985) and, in particular, the passage in the judgment of Lord Justice Robert Goff. The principle was only applied where the court was satisfied that earlier decisions were clearly erroneous by reason of some misapplication or misunderstanding of the law.

For his part, Mr Justice Dyson was wholly unpersuaded, despite the criticisms of illogicality and artificiality, that the well-established line of earlier cases, to some of which he had referred, was erroneous in law. It was quite plain that Lord Chief Justice Widgery, in particular, had on several occasions considered the matter very carefully, alive to the criticisms, and had decided to maintain the principle.

There was, it seemed, a further restriction on the ability of the Court, in exercising its criminal jurisdiction, to decline to follow earlier authority. That arose from a consideration of *Regina v Jenkins (Edward John)* (1983) and *Regina v Spencer* (1985). Those were both decisions of the Court of Appeal (Criminal Division). In particular, he had in mind a passage in the judgment of the court in *Regina v Spencer*, given by Lord Justice May, where it was clearly stated that it was not sufficient for the court to be satisfied that an earlier decision was erroneous by reason of misapplication or misunderstanding of the law. An earlier decision would not be followed only if that earlier decision was adverse to the interests of a defendant in a criminal case.

Since that additional condition was not satisfied in the present case, that, in his judgment, was an additional reason for declining the invitation to depart from the well-established line of authority.

More flexible approach to the meaning of "use"

Mr Justice Dyson now turned to the two recent cases which, according to the appellants, established that the courts now adopted a more flexible approach to the meaning of the word "uses" in the context of this legislation. The first was the decision of the Court in *NFC Forwarding Ltd v Director of Public Prosecutions* (1989), a case involving a trailer. The defendant company were the owners of the trailer, which was being drawn by a tractor unit owned by a firm called Gorry and Sons and driven by that firm's employee. The defendant company were charged, under s.40(5)(b) of the Road Traffic Act 1972, and convicted of the charge of using a motor vehicle, part of which was defective. The principal judgment was given by Mr Justice Auld and the Divisional Court, for reasons which were immaterial for present purposes, found that the defendant company had been wrongly convicted. Mr Justice Auld went on, however, to make some observations on the question of the meaning of the word uses.

> *Whether or not the word 'uses' in relation to a motor vehicle should continue to be limited in this way, there is no basis on authority or logic for applying it to the offence of using a defective trailer under section 40(5)(b). So far as I am aware, there is no authority at all as to the meaning of the word 'uses' in relation to a trailer under this provision. Clearly, a different test from that applicable to a motor vehicle must be applied where a defective trailer is being drawn on the road by someone else's motor vehicle or left unattached in the road.*

It was clear that Mr Justice Auld recognised that the established line of authorities did give the limited interpretation on the word uses to which he had referred. He felt able to distinguish between the use of a motor vehicle and the use of a trailer under the relevant provisions. It was unnecessary for him to express any view as to whether such a distinction was sufficient for the purposes of the interpretation of the meaning of the word uses. Suffice it to say that the present case was not a trailer case and all that Mr Justice Auld was saying was that in his opinion a more relaxed approach to the meaning of the word uses should be adopted in the case of trailers. He was very careful not to seek to define or to provide a test for the meaning of uses in that context.

It seemed to him, therefore, that that authority really did not assist the appellant at all.

The appellant placed greater reliance upon the second authority which was *Hallett Silberman Ltd v Cheshire County Council* (1993). They said that in reality the facts of that case were indistinguishable from the facts of the present case. That case concerned a combination of a motor vehicle and trailer. The relevant facts were that the defendant company owned and operated trailers for the purpose of supplying road haulage services with abnormal loads. They had notified the prosecuting highway authority, pursuant to Article 26(2)(b) of the Motor Vehicles (Authorisation of Special Types) General Order 1979, of the movement of an abnormal load on a trailer. On the day and on the road notified, the authority's Trading Standards officer stopped the vehicle and trailer, both bearing the defendant's name, which exceeded the maximum laden weight permitted by regulation 76(1) of the Roads Vehicles (Construction and Use) Regulations 1986. The vehicle pulling the trailer was owned by the driver, who had a two-year contract to pull the defendant company's trailers; the vehicle was not that specified in the movement notice but had been included in the vehicles nominated in the indemnity provided by the defendant company pursuant to Article 26(2)(a) of the 1979 Order. The highway authority laid an information (accusation) alleging that the defendant company used on a road a heavy motor vehicle drawing a wheeled trailer when the total laden weight exceeded the maximum permitted laden weight specified in the 1986 Regulations. The defendant company was convicted and the appeal was dismissed.

The principal judgment was given by Lord Justice Beldam. He reviewed the line of authorities to which reference had been made. It was quite clear that he felt out of sympathy with the reasoning that lay behind those authorities. For example, however, he said:

> *a person can at the same time be a person who uses and a person who causes or permits another to use. Nor does it follow that two persons may not in relation to a particular use both be persons who use. Causing or permitting another to use the vehicle on the road could be given adequate scope in defining secondary or accessory liability without unduly reducing the attitude of the ordinary English word 'use'.*

He also said:

> *to determine the nature of an offence of using a vehicle in breach of regulations, it is not only necessary to consider the words and import of*

> the regulations which makes the user unlawful but also permissible to have regard to the fact that they are more likely to be aimed at visiting primary responsibility on the person who is in a position to exert influence and control in preventing the threat to public safety which it is the purpose of the legislation to deter.

He then went on to refer to Article 26(2) which had already been mentioned. The essential part of his decision started where he said:

> The defendants further contend that the self-employed driver of the drawing unit should be regarded as the sole user of the combination of vehicles. The defendants could only be properly charged with causing or permitting the use of the combination of vehicles by the driver, Mr Keeling. But on the present restricted meaning of the word 'use', it could equally as well be argued that Mr Keeling caused or permitted the defendants to use his vehicle as that they caused or permitted him to use the trailer. Nor does it follow that there can be only one user of the vehicles which make up the combined vehicle being used in this case. Thus it seems to me that in some regulations at least the words 'person who uses a motor vehicle' are intended to cover a person whose vehicle is being used for his purposes and on his behalf, under his instruction and control, and that, from the many complex factors which a court should take into account in deciding whether a person was using the vehicle on the road, it is too restrictive to isolate the terms of the particular contract under which the driver happens to be engaged to perform the duty of driving as determining the question. In the present case, the driver, Mr Keeling, though self-employed and providing the towing unit as part of the combination of vehicles, was not responsible for selecting the route, deciding the load, loading the trailer, deciding which trailer should be used, giving indemnity or the notice of movement. His use on the road of his own vehicle was authorised by the Secretary of State notwithstanding that it did not comply with the construction and use regulations, provided the conditions were complied with. It became unlawful when used in combination with the trailer only when the maximum train weight was exceeded and the requirements of Article 26 of the Order of 1979 had not been complied with. For these two failures the defendants were responsible. The defendants owned the trailer, were responsible for loading and for overloading the combination of vehicles.

> The defendants were responsible for the failure to comply with the requirements of Article 26 and accepted that they were using the vehicle in the sense set out in the answer to the inquiries. It would seem the reverse of the intention of the legislature if in such circumstances Mr Keeling alone was to be regarded as primarily liable but the defendants liable only in a secondary sense, the more so if the reason for the creation of offences of strict liability is to put pressure on the thoughtless and inefficient to do their whole duty in the interests of public health or safety. I would therefore hold that, on the facts found by the justices in the present case, they could properly hold that the defendants used the combination of vehicles specified in the information within the meaning of section 42(1)(b) of the Road Traffic Act 1988.

The appellant had stated that that case was not materially distinguishable from the present case, and that if Lord Justice Beldam had been following and applying the principle stated in the line of authorities, then he would have been bound to allow the appeal. It was, however, highly significant that Lord Justice Beldam did not purport to depart from the long-established line of authorities or say that in his view they were wrongly decided. Had he done so, in his judgment, he would have been wrong. It was clear that he did not like the principle stated in the line of authorities, and he did not purport to distinguish it.

With the greatest respect to him, Mr Justice Dyson had found some difficulty in analysing the reasoning in Lord Justice Beldam's judgment, to see how it squared with the principle stated in the line of authorities, given that Lord Justice Beldam did not purport to state that the principle was wrong. Be that as it may, it seemed to him that there were features in the *Hallett Silberman* case which were special and which, on the facts, led the Divisional Court to reach its decision consistently with the principle stated in the line of authorities. In particular, the vehicle in question was a combination vehicle and the defendants regarded themselves as users for the purpose of Article 26(2) of the Motor Vehicles (Authorisation of Special Types) General Order 1979, that was to say for the purpose of giving the appropriate indemnity. Those facts were, in his judgment, sufficient to enable the Court to treat that as a special case.

He did not read Lord Justice Beldam as purporting to lay down some new and more flexible principle which was inconsistent with that laid down in the line of authorities.

He had come to the conclusion that the appellant did not derive any relevant support from either of the two recent authorities and that this Court should follow the well established principle. He could see nothing in the facts of this case which, if that principle was properly applied, could properly have led the magistrates to arrive at a conclusion other than that at which they arrived.

He therefore concluded that they were correct in finding that the defendant company did not use the transporter.

CASE 19: IT IS NOT NECESSARY TO PROVE THAT THE CODE OF PRACTICE FOR DYNAMIC AXLE WEIGHERS HAS BEEN COMPLIED WITH TO OBTAIN AN OVERLOADING CONVICTION

G E Curtis Heavy Haulage Limited and Michael Lesley Blackburn v the Vehicle Inspectorate and Heanor Haulage Limited v the Vehicle Inspectorate (3 January 1997)

The Queen's Bench Divisional Court ruled that in overloading cases the prosecution do not have to prove that the *Code of Practice for Dynamic Axle Weighing Machines* has been complied with in order to obtain a conviction.

G E Curtis Heavy Haulage Ltd, and one of the company's drivers, and Heanor Haulage Ltd had appealed against their convictions on overloading offences by the Wetherby, North Yorkshire, magistrates.

Giving judgment, Lord Justice Kennedy said that in each case the offence charged was using a goods vehicle on a road when the sum of the weights transmitted to the road surface by the wheels of the vehicle exceeded the authorised figure for that vehicle, contrary to regulation 80(1)(b) of the Road Vehicles (Construction and Use) Regulations 1986 and s.41B of the Road Traffic Act 1988. Regulation 80(1)(b), so far as was relevant, read:

> *no person shall use, or cause or permit to be used, on a road a vehicle for which a plating certificate has been issued, if any of the weights shown in column (2) of the plating certificate is exceeded.*

Section 41B merely made the contravention of the Construction and Use Regulations an offence.

The first case

In the first case an articulated vehicle belonging to G E Curtis Heavy Haulage Ltd and driven by Michael Leslie Blackburn on 15 December 1994 was weighed on a dynamic axle weighbridge at Boston Spa under the supervision of an enforcement officer, Mr Pollard, and was found to be 7.5% in excess of its maximum permitted train weight. As a result, both owner and driver appeared before the magistrates and were convicted.

OVERLOADING

A dynamic axle weighbridge is a narrow bar level with the adjoining surface. A vehicle to be weighed is taken across the bar and each pair of wheels is thus weighed; by adding the totals of the weighings together, the total weight of the vehicle and trailer can be ascertained.

Under the supervision of an operator, the weighbridge computer mechanism produces a printout. The evidence before the magistrates showed that Mr Pollard, having checked the printout, also checked the information which his colleague had written on to a Certificate of Weight of the type prescribed by the Weighing of Motor Vehicles (Use of Dynamic Axle Weighing Machines) Regulations 1978. Mr Pollard then served a copy of the Certificate on the driver.

At the hearing before the magistrates, that Certificate of Weight was produced by Mr Pollard to prove the offence. By virtue of regulation 4 of the 1978 Regulations, a weight determined by a dynamic axle weighbridge was presumed to be accurate to the extent of plus or minus 150kg per axle. Mr Pollard was not present when the weighbridge had originally been installed and tested, assuming that it was tested at that stage. Nor was he present on any occasion when it was tested subsequently, but the magistrates were satisfied, as a result of his evidence, that the weighbridge calibrated itself. The appellants claimed that that was achieved by what really amounted to a formal simulation which the court should regard as being of relatively little assistance, but it was quite clear that the weighbridge did have within it a self-checking mechanism for some of its functions.

As to the value as evidence of the Certificate produced by Mr Pollard, it was necessary to turn first to s.79(4) of the Road Traffic Act 1988. That section, so far as was relevant, read:

> *A certificate in the prescribed form which:*
>
> *(a) purports to be signed by an authorised person, and*

and by virtue of s.78 it was clear that Mr Pollard was an authorised person. The section continues:

> *(b) states, in relation to a vehicle identified in the certificate, any weight determined in relation to that vehicle on the occasion of its being brought to a weighbridge or other machine in pursuance of a requirement under section 78(1) of this Act*

and this vehicle had been so brought. The section says that this:

> *shall be evidence... of the matter so stated.*

So on the face of it the Certificate was evidence of its contents.

Section 79(1) also had some bearing. It provided:

> *Where a motor vehicle or trailer is weighed under section 78 of this Act, a Certificate of Weight must be given to the person in charge of the vehicle, and the certificate so given shall exempt the motor vehicle and trailer, if any, from being weighed so long as it is during the continuance of the same journey carrying the same load.*

That accounted for the conduct of Mr Pollard in handing the Certificate of Weight to Mr Blackburn after the weighing had taken place.

It was necessary, however, to go back to s.78 to look at subsection (5), which, so far as was relevant, read:

> *Regulations under subsection (1) above may make provision with respect to....(b) the limits within which, unless the contrary is proved, any weight determined by a weighbridge or other machine for weighing vehicles is to be presumed to be accurate for the purposes of any provision made by or under this Act.*

That was the provision which enabled the making of the Weighing of Motor Vehicles (Use of Dynamic Axle Weighing Machines) Regulations 1978, which indicated that the reading was to be regarded as accurate to the extent of plus or minus 150kg per axle.

In the first case, although the trailer was fitted with a compensating axle mechanism, the distribution of weight between the axles appeared to be uneven when the various axles were weighed. The court accepted Mr Pollard's explanation for this apparent variation: during his eight years of experience as an enforcement officer he had found that such variations between axles were a regular occurrence, and were often caused by a fault on the compensating axle's mechanical suspension and did not suggest a fault in the weighbridge.

The second case

In the second case, the vehicle belonged to Heanor Haulage Co. Ltd and was driven by a Mr Dimon. It was stopped on 30 March 1995 and was weighed, as it happened, on the same weighbridge that was used in the first case. The enforcement officer was a Mr Docherty, and it appeared to him that the vehicle was both overweight and too long. In fact had it not been, as was pointed out by the appellants, for those factors

OVERLOADING

which took it outside the exemption which otherwise would have applied to it, it would not have been so overweight as it turned out to be. But when the normal provisions were applied to it, it was found by the weighbridge to be overweight to the extent of 98.5%, which was somewhat alarming.

In relation to the hearing of that case, the magistrates said:

> *The second and third axles of the three-axled motor vehicle formed a compensating axle arrangement. Axles one and three and all the trailer axles were found to weigh under 12,500 kilograms each which is the maximum permitted weight for each axle which is purporting to operate under a Special Types General Order Category 2 plate. Axle number two weighed 13,290 kilograms. Measurement of the rearward projection which was not correctly marked produced a finding which took the vehicle outside the scope of the Special Types General Order and in its own right would have made the vehicle subject to the Road Vehicles (Construction and Use) Regulations 1986.*

In that case, as in the first case, a Certificate of Weight was produced at court by the enforcement officer. The Certificate had been prepared and signed by a police constable, who was the person authorised to operate the weighbridge. The magistrates accepted that the axle compensator appeared to be working and that the weight would vary from yard to yard, foot to foot, while travelling on the road. That, it seemed, was the explanation which they found acceptable in relation to the readings recorded.

No evidence that the weighbridge was operating correctly

Put shortly, the appellants' point was that in neither case was evidence produced to show that the weighbridge was operating accurately. There was no oral evidence to show that the weighbridge had been tested before being or at the time of being installed, nor was there any evidence to show that it had been tested at any stage thereafter. Reliance was placed simply upon the Certificates already referred to. The Court's attention was drawn to the code of practice in relation to such weighbridges entitled *Code of Practice for Dynamic Axle Weighing Machines*, which was produced by the Department of Transport. The introduction read:

> *The object of the Code is to provide operators, drivers and road traffic enforcement officers with information on the correct setting-up and operational use of dynamic axle weighing systems. This Code supple-*

ments The Weighing of Motor Vehicles (Use of Dynamic Axle Weighing Machines) Regulations 1978.

In paragraph 4 of the Code there appeared under the heading "Verification Procedure" the following paragraph.

Each Dynamic Axle Weigher shall be the subject of the following test procedure to establish initial acceptability and continuing accuracy.

> *(a) Each machine should be the subject of an initial test at the manufacturers premises. The test shall be conducted in the statutory mode to the full capacity of the equipment. The digital read out and tally roll printout shall be checked at 1 tonne intervals and should be accurate within a tolerance of + or - 10kg.*
>
> *(b) The machine shall thereafter be installed at the proposed weigh site observing the procedure set down in Paragraph 5 hereafter.*
>
> *(c) A dynamic weigh test shall then be conducted by a qualified Inspector of Weights and Measures in the following manner using three loaded vehicles being 2 axled rigid, and 4 axled rigid and 4/5 axle artic...*
>
> *(d) The dynamic weight test set out at (c) above shall be carried out at not greater than 6 monthly intervals when the machine is in use.*
>
> *(e) The certificate of test (Appendix 1) shall be signed by the testing officer being a qualified Inspector of Weights and Measures on completion of the test. The certificate should be retained together with the printroll for each test as an indication of the machine's accuracy valid for the ensuing period of no more than 6 months.*

The appellants' submission, as Lord Justice Kennedy understood it, was that without evidence of the testing history of the weighbridge, the prosecution evidence brought before the magistrates was incomplete. In the light of the express statutory provisions to be found in s.79(4) and s.78(5) of the 1988 Act, he was unable to accept that submission. He had no doubt that the code of practice was an important document in its own right, but nothing in it made proof of testing history a prerequisite to a conviction in this class of case. That, as it seemed to him, had already been made abundantly clear by a decision of the Court to which they had helpfully been referred in the case of *Cormac Leonard v The Vehicle Inspectorate*, decided on 5 February 1996. The issue was dealt with by Mr Justice Blofeld, who said:

> for my part, I would agree with Mr Kerl's submissions that that Certificate, ie the certificate which came into existence in that case pursuant to section 79(4) 'by itself would be sufficient evidence, unless the contrary is proved, for a court to act upon'.

The appellants had invited the Court to regard that decision as mistaken, and therefore not to be taken as a precedent. They claimed that otherwise those who operated haulage vehicles were put in something of a dilemma: they simply did not know whether or not a weighbridge was accurate and yet they had to face charges which could ruin their business. The dilemma which they faced is understandable, but the reality was that a haulier knew or ought to know when his or her vehicle was overweight. It was interesting to observe that: in the first case, when challenged the haulier was unable to explain why his vehicle was overweight; and in the second case, the driver behaved in a way which suggested that he was aware that he was not complying with the regulations with which he should have been complying.

Findings of the court

It was against that background that Lord Justice Kennedy looked at the questions which were posed in each case for the consideration of the Court. The questions were largely identical and thus it was possible to deal with the two cases together.

The first question posed in each case was: "Were the magistrates entitled to find that the contents of the Certificate of Weight, produced by the prosecution, was admissible evidence?"

The answer to that question must be both in the affirmative and concealed by the appellants. What the appellants submitted was that it was admissible evidence but incomplete evidence.

The second question was: "Were the magistrates entitled to find that the requirements of s.69 of the Police and Criminal Evidence Act 1984 did not have to be fulfilled in relation to the Certificate of Weight?"

Again there was no real issue about that. Section 69 of the Police and Criminal Evidence Act 1984 applied in relation to a document produced by a computer. The Certificate of Weight was not produced by a computer, and so s.69 did not have any application to it.

OVERLOADING

The third question in relation to the first case was: "Did the fact that an axle compensating device was fitted to the vehicle, and yet a significant difference in axle weight was shown by the Certificate of Weight, provide sufficient evidence for the magistrates to find that there was a reasonable ground for suspecting that the weighbridge was inaccurate, due to operator error or otherwise?"

That seemed to him to be somewhat unhappily worded and he would prefer to substitute for the words "provided sufficient evidence for" with the word "required". The fact that the axle compensating device was fitted to the vehicle and yet a significant difference in axle weight was shown by the Certificate of Weight did not, in his judgment, require the magistrates to find that the weighbridge was inaccurate. This was because they had the evidence of Mr Pollard as to the possible reason for that discrepancy, and they accepted Mr Pollard's explanation.

In the second case the equivalent to question three was in a somewhat different form and read: "Should the fact that a compensating axle device was fitted to the vehicle have altered the magistrates' finding that the second axle was overweight, bearing in mind the provisions of regulation 80(2) of the Road Vehicles (Construction and Use) Regulations 1986?"

The position, as it seemed to him, was not so clear in relation to the second case. There was a compensating axle device, which the magistrates accepted appeared to be working properly. In those circumstances it might be that question three gave rise to a real issue but, as it turned out, it was an issue which was of no consequence because, as the appellants accepted, the vehicle was in fact too long, and, because it was too long, it was brought back within the scope of the Construction and Use Regulations. He therefore regarded question three as academic in the circumstances and a question to which it was unnecessary for them to provide an answer.

Question four in the second case was: "Could the magistrates be satisfied beyond reasonable doubt that an offence had been committed where as a fact a compensating axle device was fitted, so the weight exerted by each axle would not necessarily remain constant?"

It seemed to him that the answer to that question must be in the affirmative.

Question four in the first case and question five in the second case were identical and read:

"Given that the prosecution did not adduce any other evidence, in the form of a certificate or otherwise, to show that:

    (i)   *the weighbridge was functioning correctly, and*

> (ii) the Code of Practice for the Use of Dynamic Axle Weighbridges had been complied with

were the magistrates provided with further sufficient reason to find that the weighbridge was inaccurate, due to operator control or otherwise?"

In his judgment the answer to that question was in the negative.

Question five in the first case and question six in the second case were also identical and read:

"Was the evidence of a single Vehicle Inspectorate traffic examiner, who:

> (i) could not witness the member of staff operating the machine whilst walking the vehicle across the dynamic axle weighbridge
>
> (ii) could give no evidence of having tested the accuracy of the weighbridge
>
> (iii) could not give direct evidence as to whether the Code of Practice for the use of Dynamic Axle Weighbridges Paragraph 4(c) and (d) was followed when the machine was tested, and
>
> (iv) was not the author of the details contained in the Certificate of Weight

sufficient to allow the Respondent to rely on the accuracy of the Certificate of Weight?"

The answer to that question, in his judgment, must be in the affirmative.

The meat of this case was really in the submission that without evidence of the weighbridge operating accurately, the evidence for the prosecution would be insufficient for a conviction. That, in the light of the provisions of s.79(4) and s.78(5), he did not accept.

Concurring, Mr Justice Mance said that he agreed with the reasons and answers given by Lord Justice Kennedy. Both cases concerned reliance by the prosecution on certificates issued by an authorised person under s.79(4) of the Road Traffic Act 1988, and they did not concern computer printouts. The authorised person in question had actually performed the functions referred to in s.78 of that Act and the weighing took place in accordance with his instructions pursuant to paragraph 3 of the Weighing of Motor Vehicles (Use of Dynamic Axle Weighing Machines) Regulations 1978, which related to s.78(1) and s.79(4) of the Road Traffic Act 1988. It seemed to him irrelevant that the authorised operator did not in fact perform other functions, such as actually operating or testing the weighbridge.

OVERLOADING

Under s.79(4), the Certificates in those circumstances became evidence of the weight determined which was taken in each case from a printout from the weighing machine computer. They were, however, only evidence within certain limits, plus or minus 150kg, because regulation 4 under s.78(4) so provided. As evidence in each case the Certificate could of course have been challenged by contrary evidence, for example adduced by the defendants. Likewise, under s.78(5) there was express reference to a defendant's right to prove the contrary of the presumption introduced by a combination of that subsection and regulation 4.

The weight determined by a weighbridge or other machine, which was referred to in s.78(5), was clearly the actual weight so determined. Likewise in section 79(4) that was also the obvious effect of the form prescribed by regulation 5, which was duly used in each of the cases before the Court.

The appellants' submission was that the phrase "weight determined" in section 79(4) meant merely that a Certificate of Weight under that subsection was evidence of a printout, which would then itself require to be adduced and proved in some other way, for example under s.69 of the Police and Criminal Evidence Act 1984. That submission was clearly wrong; the certificate under s.79(4) was direct evidence of the actual weight, although not of course conclusive and always subject to the degree of tolerance allowed by s.78(5) and regulation 4 and further always subject, under s.78(5), to any contrary evidence.

The appellants had submitted that it was incumbent on the prosecution to produce evidence of compliance with the *Code of Practice for Dynamic Axle Weighbridges*, which stated that its object was: "to provide operators, drivers and road traffic enforcement officers with information on the correct setting-up and operational use of dynamic axle weighing systems", and then went on to say that it supplemented the regulations to which he had referred.

An obligation on the prosecution to establish compliance with the code of practice would in fact be a most onerous and uncertain obligation if all the provisions of that code were looked at. The appellants sought to focus on the reference in paragraph 4(e) to a certificate of the machine's accuracy, but the code of practice in fact went wider, covering the history and operation of the weighing machine. It seemed to him most improbable that such an obligation would have been envisaged. The true position was that the code of practice had no statutory force; it was not part of the scheme of legislation and regulations which the Court presently had under consideration. Obviously, however, it might have considerable significance as a practical matter and might in that way offer road transport operators comfort.

First, it was no doubt the framework within which Trading Standards officers inspected, tested and certified or permitted weighing devices acting under legislation, such as ss.18 and 20 of the Weights and Measures Act 1982.

Second, a road transport operator faced with a prosecutor relying on a Certificate under s.79(4) might be able to investigate the reliability of a weighing machine and might in that context be able to draw assistance on that issue from compliance or non-compliance with the code of practice. Thus the code of practice might have practical and indeed evidential significance for an operator in seeking to persuade magistrates that the evidence of the weight provided by the Certificate under ss.79(4) and 78(5) should not, in the particular circumstances of the case, be accepted. However, in the present cases there was no such evidence, and the magistrates came to the conclusion, on the evidence before them, that there was nothing to contradict or outweigh the certificates and they were fully entitled to do so.

Last, the appellants pointed out that there appeared to be no regulations relating to conventional weighbridges, that brought ss.79(4) and 78(5) into operation. Assuming that to be so, it did not appear to be of significance. There might of course be differences in reliability, as the appellants accepted, between different types of device, or there might be other factors making a distinction appropriate. It might simply be that the Secretary of State had not as yet introduced such regulations to achieve a similar position across the board. He certainly could have done. Whatever the position, there was no significance attached to the point. The primary legislation contained in ss.78 and 79 of the Road Traffic Act 1988 was what the Court had to construe, and, for the reasons give, he had no doubt that its effect was as his Lordship had stated.

INDEX

A
absolute liability 26–8
Alan Geoffrey Bird (1995) 21–2

B
Belgian Law, Article 2 1
Belgium 1, 15

C
*Carmichael & Sons
   Ltd v Cottle* (1971) 73–4
Certificate of Weight 67–9, 84,
   85, 86, 88, 89, 90, 91
*Chairman of London County
   Sessions ex parte Downes*
   (1953) 52
**Code of Practice for Dynamic
   Axle Weighing Machines** ... 83–92
   correct operation of
      weighbridge, no evidence
      of 86–8
   court findings 88–92
   *G E Curtis Heavy Haulage Ltd
      and Michael Lesley
      Blackburn v Vehicle
      Inspectorate*
      (1997) 83–5
   *Heanor Haulage Ltd v Vehicle
      Inspectorate* (1997) 85–6
computerised weighbridges ... 65–6
Connelly v DPP (1963) 52
*Cormac Leonard v The Vehicle
   Inspectorate* (1996) 67–9, 88

**Council Regulation (EEC) No.
   543/69** 5, 6, 7, 8, 11,
      12, 22
   see also Council Regulation
   (EEC) No. 3820/85
**Council Regulation (EEC) No.
   3820/85** 1, 3, 12–13, 16, 17,
      20, 44
   Article 1 .... 31, 38–9, 49
   Article 1(4) 2, 6
   Article 1(5) 16, 18
   Article 2 .... 9, 12
   Article 2(1) 9, 11, 12, 13
   Article 2(2) 12
   Article 4 49
   Article 6 .... 15, 21
   Article 6(1) 6, 7, 11, 18, 37, 39, 43
   Article 7 .... 6, 7, 21
   Article 7(1) 5, 6, 7, 8, 43
   Article 7(2) 5, 7, 8
   Article 7(5) 18
   Article 8 .... 11, 21, 37–8, 39
   Article 8(1) 9, 10, 11,
      12, 13, 15, 18, 19
   Article 8(3) 37
   Article 11 6
   Article 12 .... 6, 7, 21–2
   Article 15(1) 22
**Council Regulation (EEC) No.
   3821/85** 5, 8, 16, 19, 20,
      31, 49
   Article 2 .... 2, 18
   Article 3(1) 31
   Article 15(2) 3, 15, 16, 17, 19
   Article 15(3) 15, 16, 17, 18
   Article 15(4) 15, 18

INDEX

Article 15(7) 1, 2, 3
Court of Appeal (Criminal Division) 51–3
Crawford v Haughton (1972) 73, 74

D

daily working period 15–20
"day" 16
   definition 19–20
Director of Public Prosecutions v Cargo Handling Ltd (1991) .. 31–5
Director of Public Prosecutions v Marshall and Bell (1989) 63–4
Director of Public Prosecutions v Vivier (1992) 34
drivers' hours and tachographs 1–53
   daily working period 15–20
   driving periods and breaks 5–8
   emergency departures from drivers' hours rules 21–2
   falsification abroad 51–3
   knowledge necessary for breaches of drivers' hours rules 23–30
   "last day of previous week" definition 1–3
   "permissible maximum weight" means "gross weight of vehicle and trailer" 49
   permitting drivers' hours offences 43–7
   "roads open to public" 31–5
   tachograph falsification 51–3
   timing drivers' work and rest periods 37–9

twenty four hour period and journeys to countries not party to AETR 9–14
wilful ignorance is not "causing an offence" 41
driving periods and breaks 5–8

E

East West Transport Ltd v DPP (1995) 65–6
emergency departures from drivers' hours rules 21–2
end of working period 16
European Court 1–22

F

Forgery and Counterfeiting Act 1981 51–3
France 7

G

Garrett v Hooper (1973) 74
GE Curtis Heavy Haulage Ltd and Michael Lesley Blackburn v the Vehicle Inspectorate (1997) 83–5
Global Plant Ltd v Secretary of State for Social Services (1972) 75
Goods Vehicles (Licensing of Operators) Regulations 1995 55
Goods Vehicles (Operators Licences, Qualifications and Fees) Regulations 1984 55

INDEX

*Grays Haulage Co.
Ltd v Arnold* (1966) 27

H

*Hallett Silberman Ltd v Cheshire
County Council* (1993) 78, 80

Harrison v Hill (1932) 33

*Heanor Haulage Ltd v Vehicle
Inspectorate* (1997) 85–6

High Court of Justice
(Queen's Bench
Division) 23–49, 55–6, 57–92

House of Lords in *Regina v
Shepherd* (1993) 66, 67

*Howard v G T Jones &
Co. Ltd* (1975) 74–5

J

*J H Myers Ltd v Licensing
Authority for the North East
Traffic Area* (1988) 57–61

*J Theobald (Hounslow) Ltd and
another v Stacy* (1979) 59–60

James & Son v Smee (1955) 27

K

Kelly v Schulman (1988) 11, 37–9

*Kevin Albert Charlton, James
Huyton and Raymond Edward
William Wilson* (1993) 5–8

*Knowles Transport
Ltd v Russell* (1975) 26–7, 28

L

"last day of previous week",
meaning of 1–3

*Licensing Authority for Goods
Vehicles in the Metropolitan
Traffic Area v Patrick William
Coggins* (1985) 23–30
    tachograph records as
        admissible evidence 28–9

Light v DPP (1994) 43–7

M

*Marc Mechielsen and Geybels
Transport Services NV (GTS)*
(1994) 15–20

*Mario Nujs and Transport Van
Schoonbeek-Matterne NV*
(1991) 1–3

Montgomery v Loney (1959) ... 33–4

Motor Vehicles (Authorisation of
Special Types) General Order
1979 86
    Article 26 79–80
    Article 26(2) 79, 80
    Article 26(2)(a) 78
    Article 26(2)(b) 78

Motor Vehicles (Construction and
Use) Regulations 1986
    regulation 23 63
    regulation 66 63
    regulation 80(1) and (2) 63, 64

Motor Vehicles (Construction and
Use) Regulations 1951
    regulation 101 27

N

Netherlands 9, 10–11

INDEX

NFC Forwarding Ltd v Director of Public Prosecutions (1989)..... 77

O

operators' licensing................... 55–6
overloading 57–92
   Certificate of Weight 67–9
   Code of Practice for Dynamic Axle Weighing Machines 83–92
   computerised weighbridges .. 65–6
   conviction............................... 83–92
   owners do not "use" vehicle when driven by self-employed driver................................ 71–81
   permitted weight excess 57–61
   Road Vehicles (Construction and Use) Regulations 1986 63–4

owner does not "use" vehicle when it is driven by self-employed driver 71–81
   "narrow" meaning of the word "use" 73–6
   "use", more flexible approach to meaning of 77–81

P

period of work.......................... 16–19
"permissible maximum weight" means "gross weight of vehicle and trailer" 49
permitted weight, in excess of 57–61
permitting drivers' hours offences 43–7
Police and Criminal Evidence Act 1984
   s.69 .... 68, 88, 91
   s.69(1)............................. 65, 67, 68
   s.78(5).. 68

R

Redhead Freight Ltd v Schulman (1988) 41
Regina v Anthony Colin Osman, Richard Mills and Robert Chalker (1993) 51–3
Regina v Burnham, Bucks Justices ex parte Ansorge (1959) 60
Regina v Greater Manchester Coroner.. 28
Regina v Jenkins (Edward John) (1983) 76
Regina v Jones and others (1974) 52
Regina v Manchester Coroner ex parte Tal (1985) 76
Regina v Spencer (1985)............... 76
Regina v Tobierre (1985) 53
Road Traffic Act 1960
   s.73 27
Road Traffic Act 1972 75
   s.40(5)(b) 77
Road Traffic Act 1988
   s.41(b)... 83
   s.42(1)(b) 80
   s.78 .... 68, 85, 90, 92
   s.78(1).............................. 68, 84, 90
   s.78(4)... 91
   s.78(5)................. 69, 87, 90, 91, 92
   s.79 92
   s.79(1)... 85
   s.79(4)............... 68, 69, 84, 87, 88, 90, 91, 92
   s.108 49
Road Traffic Regulation Act 1984.. 32

INDEX

Road Vehicles (Construction and Use) Regulations 1973 58

Road Vehicles (Construction and Use) Regulations 1978 58

Road Vehicles (Construction and Use) Regulations 1986 86
  regulation 66 58
  regulation 76(1) 78
  regulation 80 57
  regulation 80(1) 57, 58, 83
  regulation 80(2) 89

"roads open to public" 31–5
  definition 32–5

S

Small v DPP (1994) 49
Switzerland 9

T

tachographs *see* drivers' hours and tachographs

Transport Act 1968
  s.60 55
  s.96 .... 24–5, 26, 27, 43, 44
  s.97 .... 26, 41, 49

Travel-Gas (Midlands) Ltd v Frank Reynolds and others (1988) 57–61

twenty four hour period and journeys to countries not party to AETR 9–14

U

United Kingdom 7, 16

V

Van Swieten BV (1994) 9–14, 19

W

weighbridges, computerised ... 65–6

Weighing of Motor Vehicles (Use of Dynamic Axle Weighing Machines) Regulations 1978 .... 84, 85, 87, 90
  regulation 4 .... 69, 84

Weights and Measures Act 1982
  ss.18 and 20 92

West Yorkshire Trading Standards Service v Lex Vehicle Leasing Ltd (1995) 71–81

wilful ignorance is not "causing an offence" 41

Windle v Dunning & Son Ltd (1968) 73

Wing v TD and C Kelly Ltd (1996) 55–6

work and rest periods, timing of 37–9